LOST LOVE

Nicole J. Roney

Contents

Going Back

MADELINE POV

I sat on the cold floor as I stared out at the window and took in the beautiful landscape of New York City. It was so dark outside that the city lights were the only thing you could see now. I had always been fascinated by the gorgeous view of the city at night but right at this moment I couldn't care less, it didn't look extravagant anymore.

I just felt numb. Today I had lost my mother, my boyfriend, and the people I called my family. I had lost it all in a matter of minutes.

I curled up in a ball with my legs against my chest as I began to cry once again.

Suddenly I felt someone rub my back and I knew William had come back. We were staying at a hotel at the moment and he had left to bring us food.

"It's going to be alright Madeline. I'm here for you." I turned around and embraced William. I needed to feel someone's warmth, maybe this would help relieve the empty cold feeling I felt.

William was a sweet guy but I couldn't help but crave Grayson's touch and his warm embrace. It was hard to admit it but Grayson was the only person who could make me feel protected in his arms. I missed him so much. But it was because I loved him so much that it hurt me the most when I found out the news. He had kept it away from me for so long.

It felt like so many emotions were swirling through my mind. I was grieving for the loss of my mother and a family I still loved.

It felt like I had been crying for hours and suddenly I was able to calm down. William held me in his arms the entire time letting me know he was here for me.

Finally we both stood up and I walked over to the bed to sleep.

"You're not going to eat?"

"I'm not hungry." I didn't feel like eating. I just wanted to sleep forever. Maybe if I was fast asleep I wouldn't feel this pain in my chest. This sadness could possibly go away and I could be at peace for just one moment.

William grabbed my hand.

"Please Madeline, come and eat. You're going to get sick if you stop eating." He was right. I couldn't be so stubborn as to let my health waste away from this sadness.

But it was so difficult. I felt this pain on my chest and this overwhelming feeling of sadness.

William practically had to force me to eat but I did. He had brought us some sandwiches and I had only taken a bite before heading back to bed. I layed down and continued to cry once again. William sat beside me patting my back until I finally fell asleep.

5 years later-----------------------------------

I walked downstairs to grab my bag and I headed out. I currently work for my Grandfather's company. Leclaire Enterprises is well known as a textile company with chains around the world. Although currently I work at their company in England where my grandparents are staying at.

After my high school graduation my grandparents came to look for me at the Lockwood family household. But they didn't find me there. William came in contact with Grace and luckily my grandparents were able to find me in the hotel I was staying at with William.

It was a complicated reunion. I resented them for never having visited me before. But it felt good to be near my grandparents since I could see my mother's face in them. My mother had the same blonde hair as my grandmother and the equally beautiful blue eyes as my grandfather.

I applied to a prestigious University in England since my grandparents were currently living there. After earning my bachelor's degree in business, I began to work for my grandfather's company.

It had been almost a year now since I've started working here and I loved it.

I greeted the lady at the front desk and I headed to the elevator. As soon as I walked out I headed over to the CEO's office.

As I entered I was greeted by my lovely grandfather. I gave him a quick hug and I sat down on a chair in front of him.

"So tomorrow is the big day! You're leaving for New York." I hugged my grandfather tightly.

Our company had just signed a contract with another firm in New York. I was going to be inheriting my grandfather's company after he retired and he felt that it would be best to send me to New York as a representative of our company.

"Yes and I'm sure I'll do great. You were my teacher after all."

He had taught me all there was about our company. I was an intern at this firm and I learned a lot from him. Now it was time for me to use all of the tools he gave me to succeed in this new project.

"You've grown so much Madeline. I recall the day your grandmother and I properly met you for the first time. We couldn't help but break down seeing how much you resemble your mother. I was afraid you would resent us forever but when you began to open up to us, you have no idea how much that meant to the both of us. Now look at you, you're all grown up and now you're going to represent our company."

It had certainly been hard getting used to being with grandparents at first. But they were exactly what I needed in that moment. They won my heart and now I couldn't imagine myself being apart from them. This made it even harder to leave England.

"It's all thanks to you and my grandmother. I couldn't have accomplished any of this without your help." I smiled at him.

"Your grandmother is making ratatouille for your going away dinner. Invite that William guy your good friends with."

I had lost all ties with the Lockwood family and all their relatives except for William. He had stayed by my side all these years and he was my best friend. Although I was aware he harbored romantic feelings towards me which I never reciprocated. I've always only seen him as a good friend, nothing more.

I said goodbye to my grandfather and I began to grab some last minute items from my office. Someone else was going to come and clean up the area so I wasn't too worried.

I headed back to my apartment and I double checked to see that I had packed everything I needed for New York. Everything seemed to be in order and I checked my phone to see what time it was.

It was late meaning it was time for dinner at my grandparents house. I headed out and as I got out of my car I spotted William. He had also just arrived.

I went over to him and I hugged him.

"Hey, we arrived at the same time." I smiled.

"Great minds think alike." He answered giving me a wink. William sometimes tried to be flirtatious with me but I never paid much attention to him. He was just a good friend to me.

We walked inside and I greeted my grandparents. We all sat at the dinner table as we began to eat the amazing food my grandmother had made us. The table was elegantly arranged with fancy tableware. This detail always reminded me of Grace since she was fond of setting up the table in an elegant manner. I pushed the thought away feeling a pain in my chest thinking about her and the rest of the Lockwood family.

We ate the delicious dinner as we talked about my mother and how much I resembled her. I loved these dinners since I always learned something new about my mother. Being with my grandparents felt like I hadn't completely lost her.

As soon as we were done I gave my grandparents a tight hug as we shared an emotional goodbye.

I wouldn't be seeing them for a year. Although they did plan to visit me in New York so that made me happy.

I walked out with William. As I headed to my car I felt him grab my hand as he pulled me toward him.

"I think you might already know this but I need to say it. I love you Madeline. I've been in love with you all these years." I was aware of his feelings but it was still shocking to hear him say those words.

The only other person who had said that to me was Grayson. Why was I even thinking about him at this moment?

"I'm happy that you feel this way but I can't reciprocate. I'm leaving for New York tomorrow and I just don't believe in long distance relationships." This was an excuse. I had never felt romantic feelings toward William. Whether I was leaving or not, I would have turned him down either way.

"Madeline we've been best friends for so long now that I know you're just saying this so I won't get hurt. I know you don't feel the same way as I do and that's ok. I've always known."

I could see the sadness in his eyes. I gave him a gentle kiss on his cheek as my way of saying goodbye to him.

"Thank you for everything, I'm going to miss you." William really wanted to go with me to New York. But he was still studying to become a doctor so leaving England just wasn't a choice.

"Me too." He said.

We parted ways and I headed back to my apartment. As I Iaid in bed I realized that my life was about to change, tomorrow I would start my new life. Although I worried that my past would get to me. New York filled my mind with lots of positive and tragic memories.

I only slept for a couple of hours that night and before I knew it, I was in the airplane heading to the US. The flight was long but as soon as I arrived at my apartment it all felt better. My grandfather had picked out a great place for me. There was a large modern looking kitchen with a large living room space beside it. I hadn't even checked my bedroom yet but I was already amazed by the gorgeous view of New York city. There were large windows that showcased an amazing view. I couldn't help but look in awe.

Luckily the apartment was already fully furnished and decorated. My grandfather had paid someone to prepare the space for me. I pulled my suitcase and took it to my bedroom. It was a large room with a minimalistic feel to it. The bed covers were white and I was tempted to lay down in the comfortable sheets. There was also a large window in my room that showcased a gorgeous view of the city.

I decided to take a shower and get myself ready. It was getting dark out and I hadn't eaten anything since the plane ride.

I quickly got myself dressed and I headed out to explore the city of New York. I wasn't completely new to this city but it felt weird being back in the US after so long.

I ended up eating at a cafe. It had a cozy feel which I liked and the smell of warm hot chocolate gave me nostalgia from my time living with my grandparents. My grandmother loved to make hot chocolate from time to time and the delicious smell of it in the morning always made me happy.

After I was done, I headed back to my apartment. I felt exhausted and in need of a good sleep.

I entered the elevator and headed up to my floor. As I arrived I realized there were only two apartments on this floor. They were the largest spaces in the whole apartment complex.

I hadn't seen my neighbor all day. Although I didn't mind since I wasn't one to get too friendly with my neighbors.

As I walked through the hallway to my apartment I noticed the door open from my neighbors door. Maybe this would be a good time for me to introduce myself to the individual living in that space.

Although as soon as I realized who the person was that had just gotten out, I froze. My heart was beating so fast I felt it would come out of my chest any minute now. My hands began to tremble and my legs felt weak. I couldn't understand why this was happening to me.

Back To the Past

5 years earlier.........................

I laid in my bed as I silently cried. I couldn't remember the last time I let my feelings overtake me, maybe when I was a child I did. But nothing hurt as much as this moment.

I felt so alone being without her. Madeline was my everything and it was my fault that she was gone. I had kept her mother's death a secret for so long and now she hated me for it.

I remembered how happy she became everytime she thought she had received a letter from her mom. Her smile could make anyone feel better.

I could still remember her soft body against mine as we laid in bed. She loved to rest her head on my chest as I wrapped my arms around her. I felt like her knight protecting her from all the dangers in this world.

I missed her gentle kisses and how shy she got when I told her how beautiful she was. I noticed she wasn't used to these types of compliments. Today she had looked so ravishing and beautiful with that elegant dress she wore.

Her gorgeous hair fell gently to her sides and I was always tempted to touch it. I loved it when she put it down. Although the last thing I could remember were those tears that fell down on her cheeks. Her eyes were red as she shed tears of sorrow.

I wanted so badly to be the man she held onto. I wanted to comfort her in my arms like I had always done. But instead she had left with William.

I really wanted to beat the shit out of him for being with my woman. She was mine yet he felt he could easily touch her. In the end I had no choice but to let them go. I was crazy in love with Madeline and as soon as she told me to let her go, I had no choice but to agree.

I would respect her decision. That day I remained in my bedroom until I fell asleep.

The day that followed I tried to look for Madeline feeling determined that I could win her back. But I found out that she had left with her grandparents who knows where. My parents didn't know either.

I didn't give up and I tried to find answers to her whereabouts. Although it was all to no avail. I never found out where she left. All I knew was that she was out of the country and she was never coming back.

I felt lost and I had no energy to do anything. I remember I didn't eat much and I lost a lot of weight that year. It wasn't until my father began to get sick that I decided to push away my sadness and start picking myself up. My dad would most likely have to retire soon and I needed to be prepared for when that day came.

I attended a prestigious University in New York and I got a bachelor's degree in business. Occasionally I would go to my father's company and work for him. Now it has been almost a year that I became the CEO of Lockwood Enterprise.

My father was proud of me and his health had improved as he had stopped working.

Although after 5 years I couldn't help but still feel an emptiness in my heart. I had never let anyone else in after I dated Madeline. I became distant from my family, visiting them less and less. That home reminded me so much of Madeline.

Especially her room. My parents hadn't touched that room since she left. All of her old belongings were still here. Her lovely smell still lingered in the bedroom. That same year she left I recall sleeping on her bed as I imagined her laying beside me. I realized that she was never coming back and visiting this home would never allow me to move on.

The only way I knew how to forget about Madeline was to start seeing other people. During my time in University I played around with different women. I was known as the biggest flirt and a playboy. Although it was all just meaningless sex and no feelings attached.

I wanted to forget Madeline and this felt like the best way to do it. But no matter what I did, I couldn't forget her.

At times I found myself going back to my parents home when I felt desperate to see her. I always looked over old pictures of Madeline and I when we were children. I was afraid that I would forget her beautiful face. I recall seeing a picture of us at my aunts wedding as I stood next to her. She looked so beautiful that I took the picture and I kept it in my wallet at all times. I needed to see her and this felt like the only option.

Now that I lived alone in my apartment I had made sure to keep it that way. I still played around with different women but they never came to my home. This was my place, nobody else's.

I only ever met with them in my office, their apartment, or a hotel. At the moment I was with a hot blonde who was the daughter of an older man I worked with at the company.

She had taken a liking to me and I didn't mind the company. But I planned to break things off with us tonight. I didn't care about her and she was starting to become clingy. I really didn't need that now.

I headed out of my apartment and I heard someone's footsteps walking toward me. I was aware that there was a new tenant living next door. This would be a good time for me to introduce myself and befriend this person.

Most people that resided in this apartment complex where businesses men and other important and wealthy people. Most companies were in a special district and this building was nearby. It was a perfect living space for individuals in the business world. It's the reason I had chosen to live here.

As I looked up to face my new neighbor I immediately realized who stood before me. My beautiful Madeline, the woman of my dreams stared at me clearly in shock.

Her hair was much longer and I noticed she wore makeup now. She had always been beautiful with or without it. She wore a black dress that accentuated her small frame well.

She expressed this air of confidence and beauty. She had always expressed this but this time it felt different.

I felt enticed by her presence. Those eyes of hers that had always pulled me to her, were doing the same thing to me now.

I couldn't help but feel like the young child from before who was meeting this girl for the very first time. I recall feeling upset from the very beginning just thinking about this new girl who would be living with us. I thought my mother would love her more than me.

As soon as I looked at her I knew she was the one for me. She was so beautiful that it was difficult for me to hate her. I couldn't explain it but I wanted her.

Now she stood before me. I had imagined this moment so many times from the day she left me. I still wanted her. All of my love came crashing down and I felt like a mad man. I wanted to embrace her, touch her soft body and pull her against me as I showered her with kisses.

"Madeline" Is all I could say.

Seeing Him Again

MADELINE POV

RECAP............I entered the elevator and headed up to my apartment. As I arrived I realized there were only two apartments on this floor. They were the largest spaces in the whole apartment complex.

I hadn't seen my neighbor all day. Although I didn't mind since I wasn't one to get too friendly with my neighbors.

As I walked through the hallway to my apartment I noticed the door begin to open from my neighbor's door. Maybe this would be a good time for me to introduce myself to the individual living in that space.

Although as soon as I realized who the person was that had just gotten out, I froze. My heart was beating so fast that I felt it would come out of my chest any minute now. My hands began to tremble and my legs felt weak. I couldn't understand why this was happening to me.

END OF RECAP.......

Grayson stood before me with an equally shocked look on his face. He wore a well fitted suit and his hair was properly styled. His body was very fit and for some reason it felt as if he had grown taller. His features had matured a bit in a sexy way and he no longer looked like the clueless teenager from before. He looked like a real man now, not the young boy I once knew. He was even more handsome than I remembered him to be.

Although in that moment I realized nothing had changed. It had been 5 years since I had last seen Grayson and I still felt like that naive young girl who was blinded by love for this man.

Sudden flashes of my confrontation with Grayson 5 years ago came rushing to my head. The terrible pain I felt then hit me even stronger now. I couldn't comprehend why.

Why did all of this still hurt me? I thought I had gotten over it all but I guess I hadn't.

"Madeline" He said in a very low voice it sounded almost like a whisper.

I should have expected I would see him in New York sooner or later. I had reenacted this confrontation a million times in my head while I lived in England. I just never expected it to happen on my first day back to New York. It was like destiny was putting him in my path once again.

I looked away as I passed him. I grabbed my keys as I desperately tried to open the door to my apartment. Maybe if I pretended like I didn't know him then it would be ok. He couldn't have recognized me. I knew my appearance had also changed.

I felt someone touch my shoulder and I knew it was Grayson. I could feel his warmth. He turned me around to face him and he immediately pulled me against him as he pressed his aching lips against mine.

His strong arms were wrapped tightly on my waist as he pressed himself against me. I thought it would feel foreign being in his arms again but it felt just right.

He kissed me with desperation and longing. I planned to push him away but my body wouldn't let me. It wanted him. My arms wrapped around his neck as I felt myself move closer to him.

I kissed him back with that same yearning. Except I couldn't help but feel guilty for wanting him after all that had happened between us. He had hurt me so much and now I stood here passionately kissing him. What a hypocrite I was.

He shifted to my neck leaving warm gentle kisses.

"God I've missed you Madeline." He whispered.

He began to kiss and suck on the spot. Then he did the same to the other side. His hands roamed around my frame as he touched my body. His hands moved to my waist and went lower to my thighs and upward to my ass as he gave it a squeeze.

I suddenly moaned and it was this that snapped some sense in me.

I immediately pushed him away. My body was heated up and for some reason it felt as if I had just run a marathon. I felt agitated as I tried to calm myself down.

"I can't do this right now." I said as I turned to the door. I grabbed my keys from the floor and I quickly tried to get inside my apartment.

As I tried opening the door I noticed Grayson slammed his hand against the door, trapping me. His large body stood behind me, keeping me in that spot.

"Please Madeline, don't do this to me again." I could hear the pain in his voice.

"I don't want to talk to you." I said in a cold voice. It was hard to admit it but it hurt me to see him in pain like that. But I couldn't just forget what he had done to me.

"Madeline I beg of you. Let's talk." He whispered in my ear.

His heat and presence somewhat intimidated me. I hated feeling weak and I wasn't going to let him corner me like this.

I turned to face him.

"Fine, you want to speak to me then go ahead. Are you going to tell me the same thing as before, that you had been lying to me about my mother's death since I was a child. That you knew those letters I thought she sent me weren't really from her. How you bullied me most of my life. Made me feel unwanted and hated like my father used to. So tell me, what exactly do you want to say to me that I don't already know." I hadn't realized I was crying until I noticed the concerned look in his eyes.

"Please don't cry baby. I hate seeing you in pain."

"Oh really, because you loved to hurt me when we were kids. I don't see why that might have changed."

What was I even saying? I knew Grayson hated seeing me in pain. Even though he had disliked me when we were children, he was always by my side whenever I cried. When I had just moved in to his family's home he had slept beside me every night because I missed my mother and I wouldn't stop crying. He was the only person who could sooth my pain.

But I still resented him for keeping such a big secret from me. A secret I so desperately deserved to know. Although it was because I loved him so much that it hurt me more when I found out.

I could see the sadness in his eyes. My words had hurt him.

"Just please, leave me alone Grayson. I don't ever want to see you again." I was lying, but it hurt me so much seeing him again.

He looked as if he were on the verge of tears. Nothing came out of his mouth and instead he just left.

I finally got inside my apartment. Like a zombie I walked to my bedroom lost in thought. I laid in my bed with teary eyes. The city lights were the only thing lighting up the dark room. Then I just broke down.

I cried all night feeling this terrible pain in my chest. I hated that I saw him today. I hated the universe for putting him in my life again. But what I hated the most was that I was still madly in love with Grayson Lockwood.

I couldn't help but miss the times I slept next to him with my head resting on his strong chest as he wrapped a protective arm around me. The warmth that emanated from his body always calmed me down. Now I just felt lonely.

Going to Dinner With Him

MADELINE POV

I woke up with a huge headache. I headed to the bathroom and I took a shower. I wanted to somehow wash away the pain.

I got inside the shower and I sat on the floor. The water droplets cascaded down on my body like a waterfall. All the memories of last night hit me and I began to cry once again.

How I wished my mother was here to comfort me. I was aware that she was dead but I always felt like if I tried to talk to her maybe she would hear me from wherever she might be.

I got out and dried my hair. Then I put on some makeup and I got dressed. I had gotten in contact with my high school friend Lisa back when I was still living in England. She texted me yesterday while I was in the cafe and told me to meet with her today.

I wouldn't be starting work until tomorrow, today was Sunday and I could use this time to get familiarized with the city.

This would be good I thought. I needed to get out and have fun with my friends. I needed to forget about my past and just focus on moving forward with my life.

As soon as I headed out I couldn't help but feel a bit worried that I would bump into Grayson. Luckily he was nowhere to be found as I headed to the elevator.

Before I knew it I had arrived at a luxurious Italian restaurant that Lisa had invited me to.

"I've missed you so much Madeline. How have you been?"

Lisa didn't know anything about my fight with the Lockwood family. In fact I hadn't even told her my mother was dead. All she knew was that I left to Europe with my grandparents.

She was a friend I truly valued and I was happy we could still hang out after all these years.

We ate pasta and had some wine. The food was honestly delicious and it helped me forget my sorrows.

Lisa told me that her parents had finally divorced. I assumed she would be devastated but she claimed that her parents seemed happier this way and they were no longer fighting. She too seems very happy with the outcome.

This is what I wished for my own parents. What would have happened if my father had agreed to their divorce? Maybe I would be living with my mother right now. She would be alive and we would be much happier.

I wondered if even then I would have been close with Grace and Ian. Would I have dated Grayson? I really needed to stop thinking about him.

We said our goodbyes and I headed home. I got ready for work tomorrow. The company I was partnering with would be my new workplace.

I went to bed early since I would be waking up early tomorrow.

Before I knew it I was heading out of my apartment and heading to the company. I was excited and nervous at the same time.

I would represent my grabfather's company and if everything worked out alright then Leclaire Entreprise would be able to expand to the US.

I greeted the lady at the reception desk and she told me what floor the CEO's office was located at.

As I arrived at the top floor I was led to the CEO's office. The secretary opened the door for me and I walked in.

The door closed and I walked up to the man I would be working with. But as I stared at his features I realized I knew this man very well.

"Jack?" I said.

"Madeline is that really you?" He observed me almost like he was checking if it was really me. When he looked satisfied he walked around his desk encasing me in a hug. I couldn't help but hug him back. He had always been like an older brother to me and he always would be. I knew he felt the same way.

It felt weird and awkward seeing him again after everything that had happened with me and the Lockwood family. He was the only person in that household who didn't know that my mother had died apart from me. You could say we were both fooled.

I assumed Grace had told him everything. I mean I had left that party so abruptly, and he had especially come to see me and Grayson graduate.

I felt warm tears on my cheeks. Lately I was crying all the time and I hated it. I always felt like it was a form of weakness.

"Please sit down." I could see the concern in his eyes. He resembled Grayson a lot. They were brothers after all.

I sat down and so did he.

"How have you been?"

"I don't even know where to begin."

I told him everything that had happened. From the day of my graduation until now. Soon I would inherit my grandfather's business and I would become the next CEO.

So many things had changed in just five years. Jack also appeared different, he looked a lot older from the last time I saw him.

"I'm so sorry about what happened that day. My mom told me about your confrontation. I completely understand why you left. Although I want you to know that it truly hurt us to see you leave. You're like my little sister and to see you leave so suddenly like that really hurt. My mom was so distraught and so was my father. I'm not even going to talk about Grayson because it hit him worse than all of us. He's never been able to forget you Madeline. Even now I know you're the only one woman he will ever love. Although he's completely changed. He's much more distant and cold."

I pained me to see how much I had hurt the Lockwood family. I know they care about me just as much as I care for them. I always contemplated whether I should get in touch with them. But in the end I could never do it.

It felt like I was betraying my mother.

"I never meant to hurt anyone by leaving. But I felt it was the best decision I could make at that moment. For Grace, Ian, and Grayson, my mother had died years ago. But for me it was as if she had died on the day of my graduation. They kept that away from me for so long. I couldn't bear to see their faces. I was grieving for the loss of my mother. I needed to go with my grandparents. They are all I have left of my mother."

I realized I was crying again. I tried to calm myself down realizing that I should have been working today rather telling Jack my whole life story. Although he didn't seem to mind. I knew he cared about me.

Jack gently rubbed my shoulder.

"It's alright Madeline. I understand."

I decided to push away my personal life aside and get straight to business.

Jack gave me a breakdown of the whole company. He explained each division in the company and what they did exactly to contribute.

Grayson apparently had taken charge of Ian's company while Jack decided to start up his own business. The Lockwoods were very wealthy and they had many connections with powerful people. This helped Jack succeed in his own company.

I was then given a tour of the whole building by Jack's secretary Linda. She was a very kind woman who seemed very efficient in her work.

Everyone was very friendly and it seemed like an excellent working environment. It immediately changed my energy and I felt more positive. Everything will be alright I told myself.

I was then shown to my office where I would be working. It was a large room with a grand window that showcased a beautiful view of the city.

My shift was over and I headed out to shop for some items to personalize my office. Before I knew it I had purchased my groceries and other necessities for my apartment.

I headed into my apartment and I put everything away. I then changed into some comfortable pjs and I headed out to the balcony with a warm cup of tea and a book.

I was a hopeless romantic and most if not all of the books I read were romance novels. I sat there until I finished the whole book. Occasionally when the main characters kissed I would smile to myself like a fool. I lived for these cute moments. It was beginning to get cold so I decided to get back inside. Although not before I heard someone call out my name.

"Madeline"

I turned to my right towards the other balcony as I looked over to see a handsome Grayson. He wore a black t-shirt and matching pants.

They were a simple sleepwear set but he still looked sexy in them. I tried to clear my thoughts and stop thinking about how attractive Grayson was.

I looked away and I began to head into my apartment.

"No wait! Please let's talk!" I could hear the desperation in his voice again.

I immediately stopped as soon as he told me to wait. I turned back to face him. When he was sure I wouldn't leave he began to speak again.

"Would you like to go to dinner with me tomorrow? This way we can properly talk things through about everything."

It seemed more like a demand rather than a question. I wasn't sure if I should agree. Although there were many questions I had for him about what he knew regarding my mother and how exactly he found out about her death.

"Very well then we can meet tomorrow."

His whole energy completely changed and he gave me a dashing smile.

"Great! I'll pick you up at 8."

I simply nodded in agreement.

"By the way you have a beautiful smile." He gave me a wink as he headed back inside to his apartment.

I felt myself blushing. It dawned on me that Grayson had probably been standing there for a while as I read my book. Or had he been outside his balcony the entire time and I hadn't noticed him?

Clearly he was staring at me at some point because he saw me smiling at myself as I read my book. I hated how much his words got a reaction out of me.

I headed inside and I laid in bed. It was hard to fall asleep thinking about tomorrow. Deep inside I felt excited for this date but my mind was telling me to stay strong and not let my emotions get the best of me. I couldn't let Grayson know I'm still in love with him.

The next morning I felt extremely exhausted. No matter how hard I tried to fall asleep I just couldn't. I couldn't help but wonder how dinner would be like with Grayson. We would be seeing each other face to face again after our kiss.

I decided to push those thoughts away as I changed, ate some breakfast and I headed out.

I had arrived at Jack's office on time. We went over the details of our partnership. Each of our companies was to focus on part of the project. Luckily everything went smoothly and I headed to my office to work.

I was so engaged in my work that I didn't realize it was lunch time already. As I entered the elevator downstairs I saw Jack walk inside.He invited me to eat with him and I agreed.

We ended up eating at a nice cafe nearby. There was an assortment of pastries and the lovely smell of coffee filled the shop. We ordered our sandwiches and we sat down.

"I apologize if this question is uncomfortable for you and you want to refuse but I can't help but ask if you would be willing to come to dinner at my parents home. Grace's birthday is coming up this weekend and I think it would mean a lot to her if you could come."

I didn't know how to respond. I cared for Grace like a second mother and I would be lying if I said it didn't hurt me that she kept a secret from me for so long. Although I was well aware hom much it would mean to her if I attended her birthday dinner.

When I used to live with the Lockwood family I would always give her a special present. As a child I would draw her a picture and write her a heartfelt letter. But as soon as I got a job I would save up money to buy her a small but meaningful gift. I could never afford luxury gifts but I knew the gift that I did give her meant a lot. I guess it made her feel like I accepted her as a mother figure and she was right.

It took every ounce of courage for me to say it but I agreed. I needed to heal from the past and this was certainly a start. I was meeting up with Grayson tonight to talk about past issues, I sure could do the same with Grace and Ian.

"Thank you Madeline. I know this is hard for you but I truly appreciate that you're coming over." He smiled at me as a form of encouragement.

I smiled back feeling glad that he understood how I was feeling about all of this.

We headed back to the company and I continued to work in my office until my shift was over.

I grabbed my things and I went home to get myself ready. I took a quick shower and then I did my hair and makeup. I felt indecisive on what to wear. It felt as if I was getting ready for a date and I hated that feeling because it was Grayson I would be seeing.

I calmed myself down and I wore a well fitted black dress. It showed a bit of cleavage but I was ok with that. It was still a very elegant dress.

It was finally 8 and I headed out of my apartment. As soon as I turned around I saw a very handsome Grayson staring back at me. He seemed composed and rather serious. Although it didn't take away the fact that he looked extremely attractive in that suit. It fit him like second skin.

His hair was carefully styled and those dashing hazel eyes of his tentatively stared into mine.

"You look beautiful as always." He finally spoke.

"Thank you" Is all I said.

"Well let's get going shall we."

I walked ahead not wanting him to hold my hand as to lead me. I much preferred being alone. It's not like we were friends.

As soon as we arrived at the restaurant he opened the door for me like a true gentleman. I walked inside and I felt him touch the small of my back as we were led to our table.

He then pulled up a chair for me and I sat down. Back when we were dating he was a true gentleman, I was glad to see he hadn't changed.

"I know you're probably not comfortable being around me after what happened 5 years ago but I want you to hear me out tonight."

I simply nodded in agreement. I truly wanted to hear what he had to say. We quickly ordered our food and we began to talk.

"I found out about your mother's death no long after it happened. I was still a child with pent up issues and insecurities and I wanted to ask my parents how long you would be staying with us. But as I arrived at her door I heard them conversing about your mother. After I found out she was dead I was truly shocked. I immediately thought about you and how much pain that might cause. After you arrived at our home I made it a habit to sleep beside you so you wouldn't cry. Even then it hurt me to see you in pain. Although I honestly never planned to tell you about her death. As time passed by and we grew up I knew your connection to your mother had grown stronger. You believed you were receiving letters from your mother and I saw how happy that made you. I honestly didn't want to be the one to tell you such terrible news. I guess in a way I didn't want you to hate me. Although I know it was worse that I kept this secret from you for so long."

I could tell he was genuinely sorry. It was evident that he didn't want to hurt me, but he had. I wish he had told me my mother died as soon as it occurred. Although instead he and his parents made me feel like my mother had abandoned me by keeping that secret from me. It was still hard for me to forgive Grayson.

"Look Grayson all of this is really hard for me. Seeing you again just brings back terrible memories. I just wish you would have told me about my mother's death the moment you found out. You tried to protect me but instead you hurt me more."

I tried to breath in and out slowly. There were so many other things I wanted to say to him. I felt like screaming at him and crying at the same time. I needed to change the topic fast.

"Look maybe we can talk more about this some other time. I don't think I'm ready to talk about this yet."

He simply nodded and I felt glad he didn't push the subject.

Our food finally came and we began to eat as we drank some wine.

"I'm sorry for upsetting you. If you ever want to talk please let me know and I'd be more than happy to come to you."

I could see how hard Grayson was trying to make me happy. He didn't want to inconvenience me.

"Thank you." I smiled.

He gave me a charming smile in return and I couldn't help but feel butterflies in my stomach. What is wrong with me? I was acting like a teenager in love.

"How about we start over."

"What do you mean?" I asked him.

"How would you like to be friends. I mean we've changed so much so we can hang out and get to know one another. Of course if that's what you want."

He did have a point. We both had changed so much, those naive teenagers we were once had vanished. After 5 years apart I was honestly curious to see who this new Grayson was.

"Yes, we can be friends." Is all I said. He didn't need to know I was actually interested in spending time with him. I felt so bipolar for wanting him near yet at the same time I resented him for keeping my mother's death a secret.

I could tell Grayson was satisfied with my answer. He no longer looked tense.

"So I was curious. Do you still like to cook for fun? You always used to make lavish meals when we were teenagers."

"Why do you ask? Do you want me to make you dinner sometime?" He asked with a grin.

I realized that by me asking him about his cooking might have led him to believe I wanted him to cook for me. I began to panic not knowing how to respond to that. I couldn't let him know I was freaking out.

"That might be fun. But you're probably too busy to do something like that." He probably was super busy. Grayson was the CEO of his father business, I'm sure the man had a lot of work to do. I was amazed he had time to see me tonight.

"That's no issue at all, I can always make time for you Madeline." He gave me a wink.

This man was clearly smitten with me. To make time for me even with his busy schedule meant he truly cared to see me.

Soon we finished our dinner and this saved me from having to respond to Grayson's flirtatious gestures. We then headed back to the apartment complex in Grayson's Lamborghini.

As we got out of the elevator I heard Grayson speak.

"Would you like to come inside? We are friends now right? I can show you around my place."

This felt like a bad idea and we both knew it. I had agreed to be friends with him but I still had feelings for him. I was well aware he still loved me and this strong attraction we felt for each other was getting dangerous.

I probably should have said no at that moment. My brain kept telling me I would do something I would later regret if I did go inside, but sometimes the heart wants what it wants and I agreed to enter his apartment.

Losing Control

MADELINE POV

"Would you like to come inside? We are friends now right? I can show you around my place."

This felt like a bad idea and we both knew it. I had agreed to be friends with him but I still had feelings for him. I was well aware he still loved me and this strong attraction we felt for each other was getting dangerous.

I probably should have said no at that moment. My brain kept telling me I would do something I would later regret if I did go inside, but sometimes the heart wants what it wants and I agreed to enter his apartment.

"Sure" I didn't sound too confident with my answer but Grayson didn't take any chances and he immediately opened the door guiding me inside. He touched the small of my back once again like he had done so before. I couldn't help but feel like he needed to touch me and this was his way of relieving that need.

Although to be honest I didn't mind it. I wondered if the wine was getting to me. I had never been good with alcohol.

"Would you like something to drink?"

Grayson walked over to his mini bar as he grabbed two glass cups.

"Sure"

He poured some whiskey on both cups and he placed some ice inside. He then handed it to me and we sat down on his large sofa. I couldn't help but notice how close he had sat down next to me.

He raised his cup and I did the same as we bumped glasses.

"To our new friendship." He said.

He stared at me and drank his whiskey without moving his gaze away from me. It felt like he was a lion carefully watching his prey. This sexual tension began to arise and I suddenly felt hot.

I drank some more of my whiskey as I tried to ignore Grayson hard stare.

"Would your boyfriend be upset that you're in my apartment at the moment?"

I was surprised by his question. I wondered if this was just his way of asking me if I was seeing someone.

"No, I'm not seeing anyone at the moment."

I finally looked him in the eyes but his gaze was so intense. It was almost as if he was trying to tell me something. His eyes traveled down to my chest and went lower as they explored the rest of my body.

He then looked back into my eyes as he licked his lips.

My heart began to beat fast and I felt my body heating up.

He smiled at me and I realized he was content I wasn't seeing anyone at the moment.

"I'm also single at the moment. How funny is that." He said giving me another dashing smile.

This man was trying to seduce me and it was definitely working.

I finished my whiskey and I placed the cup on the side table near me. I then stood up staring at the beautiful window view of the city. My apartment had the same view but I couldn't help but feel it looked prettier from his apartment.

I tried to calm myself down. My whole body felt tingly and I was afraid of the feeling. I felt a thrill, fear, and excitement all at the same time.

"The view is so beautiful from here." I said trying to sound calm.

I closed my eyes as I breathed in and out. My heat was beating fast. It was a bad idea to come to his apartment.

"It truly is." I heard him say behind me.

I realized he was close to me. I could feel his body heat.

"You know what else is beautiful?" I heard him whisper in my ear. That deep sexy voice of his did things to me. I could feel his warm breath on my neck making me feel weak.

He hadn't done anything yet but it felt like my whole body was melting.

"What is?" I whispered. My eyes were still closed and I felt like my other senses were activated because of it. My breathing began to speed up as well.

He didn't answer and instead I felt him begin to caress my arms. As soon as his warm hand touched my arm I felt like shivering. It was amazing how a simple touch from him could feel so good. He then guided his hand lower as he lightly grazed my chest with both of his hands.

I felt myself gasp for air feeling his gentle caress.

His hands then when lower as he touched my thighs and then he squeezed my ass cupping it with his hands. I knew I was breathing fast now.

"This dress has been tempting me all day baby." He whispered.

He took his time feeling my ass and I couldn't deny him. It felt too good to push him away. He then guided his right hand to my core as he lightly rubbed it. I tried to contain a moan by biting my lip as soon as he did it.

His lips then began to kiss my neck. He pulled the sleeves off my dress down as he began to kiss my shoulders. He then moved to the side licking and sucking on my neck.

I bit my bottom lip trying to keep myself from moaning. I wondered why I didn't stop him. He was kissing and touching every part of my body yet I couldn't seem to push him away.

But it felt unimaginably good having him touch me like this.

I then felt him unzip my dress leaving me in just my undergarments. Although he quickly removed my underwear and bra leaving me completely naked.

"God you're so beautiful Madeline." I heard him say. He stared at me with longing, lust, and so much love.

I didn't speak, unable to from having him touch me like this.

"Turn around princess." I wasn't thinking straight. I was probably drunk at this point. But I couldn't care less at the moment because I desperately needed this man.

As soon as I turned around he wrapped a possesive arm around my waist while I put my arms around his neck. His lips immediately met mine as we began to kiss with desperation.

He put his tounge in and I followed his rythm. Grayson had always been a great kisser but today he was even better at it. It might have been the fact we had been apart for so long that made this moment more special.

It felt amazing to finally kiss this man. My whole being wanted him, desired him. He was like a drug I had been wanting to stay away from but now that I had him near I couldn't get enough of him. I wanted more, I needed more. We were practically making out at this point.

I felt his hand move down to my core as he began to rub on my sensitive area. He then inserted a finger inside me. I felt him pump it in and out of me making me moan in his mouth.

"I need to taste you my love." He whispered.

He kissed my neck and then moved even lower to my core. He licked on the spot and then he sucked on it. I began to moan again from how skilled he was with his mouth.

"Oh God!" I didn't know what to say. The things he did to me and the way he touched me was so sexual.

He then inserted a finger inside me as he continued to lick my core. Almost immediately I felt myself climax. He licked me clean and then he stood back up.

We began to kiss and I could taste my cum in his mouth making it more erotic. He squeezed my ass and then he picked me up without breaking the kiss. I wrapped my legs around him as he led us to his bedroom.

It felt phenomenal being in his arms. This man truly made me feel wanted.

He gently laid me on his bed. He took off his clothes and then he grabbed a condom, putting it on himself. We were both naked now, completely vulnerable to each other. I couldn't help but stare at his sexy abs, he had an extremely toned body.

His evident hard on made me feel somewhat happy that I could turn him on this much.

I felt him lay on me and he pressed his lips against mine. It seemed like he wanted to kiss me whenever he had the chance and I didn't mind.

"You have no idea how much I've missed you Madeline." I heard him say.

It made me happy to see how much doing this meant to him like it did for me. We weren't just strangers having a one night stand. We were two individuals who cared for each other deeply and were making love.

I knew that tomorrow I would regret this decision but for now I just wanted to love this man unconditionally.

Grayson began to kiss my neck giving it small gentle kisses. I just laid there enjoying ever minute of his sweet caresses all over my body.

He moved lower as he began to give some attention to my breasts. I felt him suck on one of my nipples and I immediately moaned.

"You're so sexy when you moan baby. I think I might lose control." He spoke in a deep raspy voice. I could tell he was turned on.

He kissed and sucked on them. It felt amazing and my body began to feel hot again.

"Please Grayson, I want you." I said to him.

He gently kissed my forehead and smiled.

"You're so beautiful my love. I feel like the luckiest man to have you here with me. I won't ever let you go."

He said it like a promise. There was so much sincerity in his eyes. I was sure he meant every word he said.

I felt him kiss my forehead again then my cheeks and finally my lips.

I then felt a hard thing press against my entrance as Grayson inserted his manhood inside me. He began to thrust it in and out making us both moan.

"I love you Madeline." I heard him say.

I still loved this man but I just couldn't say it back. It felt like I was almost going against my principles. Almost 5 years ago I had broken up with Grayson and I promised myself that I would never forgive him for what he did to me that day. I never thought I would be making love with him again. It never occurred to me that I would fall for his charms so easily.

But the thing is, I was still madly in love with him. The same sensation and emotions this man made me feel were still just as prominent as they were when we were teenagers. It was evident that Grayson still felt the same way as I did from how he touched me.

Before I knew it we had both reached our climax. We laid beside each other. My head rested on his strong chest while he gently brushed my hair. His heart was beating fast and I realized he had also been nervous about doing this.

"I love you so much princess. It was so devastating for me to see you leave 5 years ago and I honestly thought I would never get to hold you like this again. Now I wonder what I did to deserve you. You're the best thing that has ever happened to me." He kissed my head and continued to brush my hair.

His sweet words meant the world to me. I loved being with Grayson. It didn't matter where I was or what I was doing, if Grayson was by my side I would be satisfied.

I didn't answer him and instead I turned to my side and hugged this gorgeous man. He gave out a sexy laugh and hugged me tight.

"Goodnight my love."

It was like old times. Being near him felt good. His warmth had always made me feel safe and all I truly wanted was to be with this man. Maybe I was truly drunk at this point, but I couldn't be happier being in this man's arms. Although tomorrow morning I had a feeling I wouldn't feel the same.

I'm Not in Love with You

MADELINE POV

I felt strong arms wrapped around me. The bed felt comfortable and I didn't feel like moving. The person beside me smelled amazing.

I opened my eyes and it was then I realized the mistake I had committed last night. I had slept with the man I swore I would never see again. How could I have been so stupid as to even agree to enter his apartment!

Panic began to surge through me and I tried to breath in and out as I deviced a plan to get the hell out of here.

I slowly removed Grayson's arms around me. Luckily he didn't wake up. With much effort I got off the bed and I quickly ran to the living room as I grabbed my clothing. I quickly changed and I took my bag with me.

Luckily Grayson was still asleep and I made it to my apartment without him seeing me leave.

The first thing I did was shower. I laid in the tub as I let the water droplets fall on my body. I had made such a huge mistake.

Maybe I should just move out? I couldn't see Grayson again. Not after what we did last night.

I got out of the shower and I changed into a nice dress. I was supposed to go to work today and if I didn't hurry up I knew I would be late.

I quickly did my hair and makeup and I headed out.

While I was in the office I couldn't stop thinking about Grayson. I was able to forget about him as I got immersed in my work but as soon as my shift was over I began to think about him again.

He was my neighbor for crying out loud. We were bound to see each other again.

As I got out of the elevator I saw Grayson outside my apartment door.

But the elevator doors had made an obvious noise and Grayson turned around to look at me.

"My love, where have you been? You left without saying goodbye and I got worried."

There was a sound of hurt in his voice. It must have pained him not to see me when he woke up this morning. I hadn't left a note to tell him where I was going, I just simply left him. He gave me a tender smile as he walked toward me at a fast pace.

I walked toward him. He needed to know that we weren't going to be together. I had made a mistake last night and he needed to know that.

He tried to embrace me but I pushed him away.

"Yesterday was a mistake. I was drunk and I wasn't thinking straight. I should have never entered your apartment."

I could see the immediate hurt in his eyes as soon as I said those words.

"What?" I heard him say in confusion.

"I'm sorry I made you think we could get back together but that's just not possible. I don't love you Grayson."

I was lying to him.

"I love you Madeline and I know you love me too. I can see it in your eyes, your touch, and even in the way you kissed me last night. I know you love me Madeline. You're just afraid. But I promise you that I will never lie to you again. I will never make you suffer Madeline. I'll take care of you." He grabbed my hands and kissed them.

I could hear the desperation in his voice.

I pulled my hands away from him. His gentle touch made me feel weak.

"Don't touch me!" I yelled. Grayson was just as surprised as I was from my reaction

"Please Madeline don't do this. Don't push me away again. I need you Madeline, you're the only woman I want in my life. I can't give my heart to anyone else because it's yours. My body, heart, and soul belong to you. It always has."

He looked distraught. I could see how much it hurt him to see me push him away.

But I couldn't bring myself to be with him again. He had lied to me before. He hurt me and lied to my face for so long when I had trusted him. I had been vulnerable around him and he took advantage of that.

"Just leave me alone Grayson. We can't see each other again."

I walked around him as I headed to my apartment. My chest hurt and I felt like crying from seeing how much I was hurting him.

"Answer this question for me Madeline. I need you to be 100 percent honest with me. It's the last thing I will say to you. After this I promise you I won't ever speak to you or come close to you ever again if that's what you want."

I immediately turned around.

"Did you feel something last night when we made love? Did the kiss we share last night mean anything to you? Or was it all just meaningless sex to you?"

He was serious as he eagerly waited for my answer.

"I didn't feel anything. I already told you I'm not in love with you Grayson. I was drunk and that's the only reason I slept with you." There was no hesitation in my voice. I didn't want him to realize I was lying.

I knew my words had truly hurt him.

Although his expression was blank. He didn't say a word. It was like time had stopped in that very moment.

"I see how it is. I won't ever bother you again Madeline." Those were the last words he spoke before he left the building.

I walked inside my apartment feeling my whole body go weak. As soon as I laid on my bed I began to cry. I snuggled up in my blankets as I sobbed. I had pushed him away.

Everytime I thought about my conversation with Grayson all that came to mind was the pain I saw in his eyes. I hated seeing him like that. But my fear of getting hurt again was so much stronger.

It had been almost a week that I hadn't seen him. He was avoiding me. It felt lonely not seeing him around in the apartment complex. I hadn't realized how happy it made me whenever I got a glimpse of his handsome face. But what did I expect? I had told him to leave me alone and he kept his word.

"Hey is everything alright? You look a bit gloomy and tired. Are you overworking yourself?" It was Jack. We were currently having lunch together.

"Yeah just a bit. I'm a perfectionist and lately I've been going to bed late working on some projects."

I felt Jack gently rub my arm for comfort.

"Don't overdo it Madeline. Take care of your health and make sure you sleep well."

"Thank you Jack. I think I'll do just that."

I hated lying but I didn't want Jack to know that I was feeling this way because I really missed Grayson. I had pushed him away even though I still loved him. It was my fault that we were both in pain.

"Well cheer up. It's my mom's birthday today. You are going to her birthday dinner right?"

I had completely forgotten about that.

"Yes, I promised you that I would come and I'm going."

He smiled, clearly content that I would be going as planned.

"That's good to hear. She's really excited you're coming you know."

"I'm glad." I gave him a weak smile.

Soon we headed back to the company. I got a lot of work done and then I headed home to change. I wanted to wear a nice dress for the small gathering.

My heart was beating fast and I felt nervous just thinking about seeing Grace and Ian again. Just thinking about being in their home brought back good and bad memories

The Reunion

MADELINE POV

I was standing in front of the place I once called home. It felt like deja vu being here again as I knocked on the large wooden door. Except the first time I was with my mother. Now I was doing this alone.

As soon as the door opened I was greeted by the maid. She then led me to the dining room.

The interior of the house looked exactly the same as the last time I saw it.

It felt like I had been here just yesterday. Although deep inside l felt like a stranger walking into someone else's home. It didn't feel like mine anymore.

As soon as the doors opened I saw the large rectangle dinner table elegantly adorned. There was expensive silverware with a variety of dishes placed on the table.

I then looked at Grace and Ian sitting beside each other. Their faces hadn't changed. They did look a bit older but they hadn't changed much. Jack sat near his parents with his girlfriend beside him. It was the same girl I had met at my graduation party.

But then when I turned to look at Grayson sitting at the table I was surprised to see a pretty girl beside him. She had short blonde hair and wore an elegant dress. It upset me to see Grayson with another woman but I masked my irritation.

Grace stood up and walked up to me.

"It's been a while." She said smiling at me.

"You're all grown up now. Look at you, you're so beautiful Madeline. I'm sure your mother would have been very proud of the woman you've become."

I couldn't help but feel like crying. Seeing Grace again felt almost like I was seeing my mother once more.

I cleared my voice, not wanting it to sound weak.

"Thank you Grace." I gave her a quick hug and then we both sat down. I felt awkward being in this home.

"I'm very happy to see you again Madeline." Ian spoke. As I looked at him closely I realized he had aged more than Grace. But he still looked handsome as always.

"Thank you Ian. It's nice to see you again." I smiled.

We all began to eat.

"I think you've already met her before but this is Kennedy, my wife."

I was utterly shocked to hear that. I had missed Jack's wedding while I was in England. How many other important moments had I missed?

"Yes I remember you. Congratulations you two, I had no idea." I gave them a warm smile.

"Thank you Madeline. You should come over to our house for dinner sometime. Maybe you can talk to me about Jack when he was younger."

"I've got quite the stories of this man. You'll definitely be surprised." I said in a teasing manner.

"Well in that case you must come over." She said eagerly.

"Are you two working against me now?" Jack added.

We all began to laugh.

I was happy that my talk with Kennedy had lightened up the mood. Although I spoke too soon as I heard Grayson's new friend speak.

"Well then I guess it's time for me to present myself. Hello I'm Emily, Grayson's girlfriend." I suspected it but actually hearing her say it hurt me more.

"Nice to meet you." So I guess Grayson truly moved on seeing as he was dating someone now.

She seemed like a decent human being but I still didn't like her. All I could do now was give her my charming smile and act like I didn't dislike her.

I looked over at Grayson but he wouldn't meet my gaze. He was probably mad and upset with me for breaking things off with him in such a terrible way.

We all finished eating and Jack and Kennedy said their goodbyes. I planned to leave soon but Grace had asked me to stay a bit longer so we could talk. I felt reluctant to go and speak with her in private but nevertheless I agreed.

She led me to the living room and we sat down.

"I know that the last time we spoke wasn't very agreeable to you. I am well aware that it was wrong of me to keep your mother's death a secret from you. You deserved to know about it the minute it happened. All I wanted to do was protect you but now I see that I just hurt you more. I should have let you grieve back then. You should have been present during her funeral and I'm terribly sorry I didn't give you that chance. I'm so sorry for hurting you Madeline. It was never my intention to hurt you. I see you as my own daughter and all I've ever wanted was for you to be happy."

Grace shed silent tears and I realized I was doing the same.

"I'm truly happy that you came back to this home to see me even after what I did to you. But seeing you again is the best gift anyone could have ever given me."

I didn't know what overcame me to hug Grace but I did. She immediately hugged me back and it felt like being in my mother's caring arms again. I began to cry and sob like the day I found out my mother had died.

"I miss her so much Grace. I sometimes dream that she's still with me. I talk to her and I ask her for guidance whenever I'm in trouble. But it hurts not having her with me anymore." I clinged onto Grace letting all of my emotions out.

I didn't mind if I was vulnerable or weak in front of Grace. It was at this moment that I realized Grace cared for me like a mother cares for a child. Although sadly I knew it would take me a while before I could truly forgive her and Ian for what they did to me.

"You know I felt like my mother had abandoned me. For years I had secretly worried that she didn't want me because I was the daughter of a monster. Hearing that she died completely changed my mindset. I am positive she loved me and she never planned to abandon me because instead she sent me you. You are that guardian angel she sent to protect me all of these years. Thank you Grace."

She hugged me tightly as her way of calming me down. After a awhile I did calm down and I wiped away my tears.

I walked to the restroom to fix my makeup from all the crying. After I was satisfied with my makeup I headed out to say goodbye to Grace and Ian. Although as soon as I headed out of the bathroom I bumped into Grayson.

"Are you ok?" I wondered if he had seen me cry while I was talking with Grace.

"Yes I'm ok thank you." I answered.

I didn't feel like speaking with him at the moment. Especially now since he was seeing someone. I couldn't help but feel a bit jealous but it was none of my business. I had been the one to turn him down.

As I walked away I heard him speak again.

"Do you want me to take you home?"

His question made me realize he had indeed seen me cry and had probably heard all of our conversation. He was probably concerned that I would cry again in my car and maybe crash from the stress.

"I appreciate your help but I'm fine Grayson." I walked away not wanting to look back at those beautiful eyes of his. He was being so sweet yet I acted like I didn't care about him.

I was torn apart between my love for Grayson and my mentality to stay away from him for having lied to me. I didn't want to play around with his feelings and go to him whenever I felt like it. He didn't deserve that.

I gave Ian and Grace a tight hug before leaving.

"Please come back tomorrow my child. I want to talk to you about something else regarding your mother. And please stay for dinner tomorrow as well."

I was curious to see what she was planning to talk to me about. Since it was related to my mother I agreed.

"Yes of course, I'll come." I gave her a kind smile and she seemed very happy with my answer.

"I'm so happy my child."

She grabbed my hand and squeezed it as a form of gratitud.

Then she turned to Grayson.

"You should also come for dinner Grayson. It's been a long time since you've come over to see me and your father. It will be a great time for all of us to catch up on lost time."

I looked to my side as I made eye contact with Grayson. Although I quickly looked away.

"Sure, I would love that mom." He gave her a hug and then he embraced Ian.

"Well then I'll see you tomorrow my children."

We waved goodbye and Grayson and I headed into our own cars.

The ride home was quick and before I knew it I had made it to the apartment complex.

As soon as I got to the elevator I met with Grayson. It was completely quiet. After what had happened between us in his apartment I didn't feel comfortable being around him. I had practically allowed him to touch me and we made love. It was all consensual yet I didn't want to give in to my feelings.

I pushed him away out of fear that he would hurt me again. My mother had passed away and was never able to come back for me. My father was physically abusive toward me and probably hated me.

On the other hand the Lockwoods were completely different from what I knew at home with my real parents. There was no fighting. All they did was give me love and care.

I guess deep inside I was terrified that Grayson would leave me alone and that his family would stop talking to me. I didn't want to be alone, not anymore.

The elevator doors finally opened and we walked toward our apartment.

"Hey Madeline."

I turned to look at Grayson.

"If you need anything please let me know. I still want us to be friends. We are neighbors after all, we can't avoid each other forever."

He was right. I knew his family and we lived in the same apartment complex. There were too many things that linked us together. Although note to self, I would never be going into his apartment again.

"Alright, you have a point. We can be friends."

He seemed happy.

Almost immediately he encased me in a surprising hug.

I froze for a minute as I felt myself go stiff. Although I finally raised my hands up and hugged him back. He was probably saying goodnight to me this way. I would be lying if I said I hated having him against mine.

I could feel his toned body against mine. My arms wrapped around his back as his rested around my waist. It was such a simple act yet it felt so intimate.

His body heat made me feel safe. His scent was so enticing and alluring. The way he pulled me against him, it was obvious we both longed for each other.

We finally let go of each other feeling the cold emptiness of being apart.

Grayson grabbed hold of my hand and kissed it. His warm lips on my bear skin felt amazing.

"Goodnight Madeline" He said as he stared right into my eyes.

"Goodnight Grayson" I answered. We parted ways and entered our own apartments.

I took off my coat and hanged it on the coat rack. I then headed upstairs to my bedroom. I changed into my pajamas, washed my teeth, and then laid in bed with thoughts of Grayson.

I wanted to be with him. He was kind and strong, attentive and gentle with me. But why did I continue to push him away?

I went to bed feeling confused about my feelings. Maybe tomorrow I could figure it all out.

Visiting Her Grave

MADELINE POV

I sat in the passenger seat of Grayson's car. Ian and Grace sat in the back seat. We were going to the cemetery to visit my mother's grave.

It made me happy to be able to visit her, but it pained me to see that our reunion would be at her grave.

We finally arrived and I grabbed the roses I had purchased for her. They had always been her favorite flowers.

I remember a long time ago when she was alive we had passed by a flower shop. She had been so entranced by these flowers that she stopped as soon as she saw them. She said my father would get mad if she purchased them so she didn't buy them. Although every time we passed by the same shop she would stop to look at them. I still wonder if it gave her joy just staring at the delicate roses.

Just the thought that my father controlled our lives to that extent truly irritated me. I felt so much hate for him that it made me sad sometimes.

Grace led me to where my mom was at. As soon as I saw her name on the gravestone I felt my legs go weak as I sat down on the grass and began to cry.

I felt my body shaking. I knew she was dead but seeing this just made it more real for me.

I felt warm arms wrap around me and I turned to embrace Grace who was also crying.

"I'm so sorry Madeline. I didn't want you to get hurt like this, that's why I didn't plan to tell you about her death. I didn't want you to feel this much pain."

I understood her intentions but I couldn't help but still feel bad about it all. All I wanted was to hold my mother and thank her for protecting me when I was a child. She endured so much pain for me and died at the hands of a monster who I was embarrassed to call my father.

After I was able to calm down I stood up.

"Can you please let me speak with my mother alone?"

They immediately understood and they headed to the car to wait for me. I caught Grayson staring at me and it seemed as though he wanted to stay and comfort me. I would be lying if I said I didn't want him to embrace me as I cry in his arms, but I needed some time to process this situation alone.

As soon as they left I sat down on the floor and began to speak to my mother. To others it might have seemed as though I were talking to myself, but it felt comforting being able to open up with my mother here. I hoped she could hear me from wherever she was.

I knew she was still protecting me, the Lockwood family who were like my guardian angels was proof of that.

"I miss you mom. Everyday I think about you." I felt tears falling down my cheeks.

"I just feel so confused about my feelings for Grayson and the idea of letting Grace and Ian back into my life. I pushed them away for so long, but now that I'm with them again it feels so right. They're all so kind to me. They accept me for me and they have allowed me into their family again. But I find it so hard to forgive them for lying to me about your death. I felt like a fool reading your fake letters."

I was aware Grace's intentions were good. She did make me happy throughout my childhood by writing those cards regardless if they came from my mother or not. I decided I would give them a chance.

"You always told me to forgive others who have hurt me. Because in the end it will be me who will continue to suffer if I don't. My heart keeps telling me that I should give them a chance, so I will. I will try my best to forgive them and heal our relationship. I hope to see you again soon mom. I love you." I wiped away my tears and I walked to Grayson's car.

As soon as I entered the vehicle there was concern in Grayson's face.

"Are you feeling alright?" He held my hand as his way of comforting me.

"Yes, I'm doing ok. We can head to Grace and Ian's home now." I gave him a weak smile and I turned to my side as I stared at the window view.

He turned on the car and we were on our way.

Grace and Ian spoke amongst themselves but I blocked out everything. I couldn't help but continue to worry about letting Grace and Ian into my life. Seeing Grayson again was also hard to take in. I had slept with him not long after we had met again and it was getting difficult to forget him.

He also has a girlfriend meaning he probably wasn't thinking about getting back with me. I just needed to forget him and focus on fixing my relationship with his parents.

Finally we had arrived at the mansion. We all headed to the theater room as we began to watch old family videos. It was nostalgic seeing Grayson, Jack, and I as children. I was a pretty happy kid growing up, regardless of Grayson's nagging and my childhood traumas.

We all then headed to the dinning room to eat dinner. Grayson sat next to me while Grace and Ian sat in front of us.

"So how has work been Madeline? Jack tells me you are excellent to work with."

"It's been great so far. Jack is also amazing to work with. He's managed the company so well and it's been great to work with someone as hardworking as him. I am inheriting my grandfather's company so I hope that I can do my best with this partnership."

"You're working with Jack?" I turned to look at Grayson. I guess he had no idea I was working with Jack.

"Yes I am, my grandfather's company and his are working on a project together."

He just nodded taking in the information.

"Good to know" Is all he said.

We all finished our food and I realized it had gotten very late. We all headed towards the front door. I planned to go home.

"Why don't you and Grayson stay over? It's really late and I would hate for you two to drive at this hour."

I wasn't working tomorrow and Grace was right. It was pretty late. I thought about my determination to make things work out between all of us and recover my connection with Grace and Ian.

"Grace is right. You two should stay over. Your bedrooms have been left untouched, you can stay in your old rooms like old times." Ian spoke.

"I'll stay over. You're right, it really is too late to be driving."

Grace hugged me clearly, happy that I agreed to her request.

"I'll stay over too." Grayson finally spoke.

I hoped he would say no, but maybe this would be good. We could become friends and I could heal my relationship with Grayson as well.

"I'm so happy to have you two stay over!"

Grace then went over to Grayson and gave him a hug.

We said goodnight to Ian and Grace since their bedrooms were downstairs. We then headed upstairs to our rooms.

I didn't say a word to Grayson and I simply walked inside my old room. As soon as I entered it, I felt like I was still in high school. Everything had been left untouched. I went over to my closet to find some sleepwear and luckily I was able to find some that still fit me. My weight hadn't changed, I simply got even more fit over the years.

I then headed to the bathroom to wash my teeth. Grace had mentioned the maids had some new toothbrushes and other amenities for Grayson and I to use. I guess she expected we would be staying over.

I then took off my makeup and I headed to my room. But I bumped into Grayson along the way. I wondered if he had been waiting outside for me the entire time.

"Hey can we talk?" Grayson asked. He wore a fitted gray t-shirt that allowed me to see his toned muscles and he had on some black pajama pants. His hands were in his pockets as he leaned against the wall.

"Sure" I answered.

"Do you want to come in?" He pointed to his bedroom.

This moment reminded me of the day he asked me to enter his apartment. I didn't want to end up sleeping with him again so I asked if my bedroom would be ok.

"How about we go to my bedroom to talk?" I very much preferred having him in my room. I guess I felt more secure since it was my property.

Although as soon as we walked inside I realized it had also been a mistake. It was my bed and this room where we made love for the first time. This bedroom held a lot of good memories for both Grayson and I.

"Take a seat wherever you'd like." I didn't have any chairs so he sat on my bed.

I sat next to him keeping some distance.

He carefully observed the room and then looked at me. He gave me a dashing smile and I couldn't help but smile back.

"What is it?" I asked.

"It's good to have you back Madeline. I really missed you."

I was surprised to see him be so open about his feelings.

"I haven't been back here for a long time. Ever since you left, it's made it hard for me to come back. I know it hurt my parents that I was staying away but it was killing me not having you close to me. Every room in this mansion reminds me of you Madeline."

He moved closer to me without keeping his eyes away from me.

"Seeing you today at the cemetery crying for your mom was difficult to watch. I wanted to keep you in my arms and whisper soothing words in your ear. It took everything in me not to embrace you. But I didn't want to make you feel uncomfortable."

He was being open and honest about his emotions while I kept denying how I felt. Why was I doing this to myself?

Grayson reached out for my hand and I didn't push him away. His large hand encased mine and it felt good.

I looked up to face Grayson. Neither one of us spoke. He moved closer toward me until our faces were mere inches apart.

I couldn't make reasonable choices whenever I was near this man. My heart was beating fast having him so close.

He began to gently brush my hair and then moved lower as he caressed my cheek. I closed my eyes feeling his tender touch. I loved it when he touched me.

"You're so beautiful Madeline. I always find it difficult to control myself whenever I'm around you." The sound of his husky voice was so hypnotic. I felt like I wouldn't be able to disobey him even if I tried.

I then felt him touch my lips as he began to rub his finger on it.

I opened my eyes to see a very desperate Grayson. He bit his bottom lip as he stared at mine.

He then looked into my eyes almost as if he were asking for permission to kiss me.

I didn't say anything as I watched his next move. He began to lean in and I closed my eyes as soon as I felt his tender lips on mine. It was like something ignited within him because he began to speed up the kiss.

He grabbed my legs and pulled me on top of him. My body faced him as he held me tightly against him.

His hands roamed around my waist and ass. Everywhere he touched me felt hot.

His tongue played with mine as he dominated my mouth. Occasionally he sucked on my bottom lip. I couldn't think right when he kissed me like this.

I felt him squeeze my ass again as he began to press his manhood against my core. I could feel his hard-on touch my sensitive spot and I couldn't help but moan. We were practically dry humping at this point.

I felt a bit worried that Grace and Ian would be able to hear us but I didn't want Grayson to stop touching me.

I pulled away to try and regain my breath.

Although Grayson didn't plan to stop anytime soon and I felt him kiss my neck. He licked and sucked on the spot. I tilted my head giving him more access.

I closed my eyes feeling all of these amazing sensations. I didn't want him to stop. He was a master at dominating my body and I surrendered to him.

He began to suck harder on my neck and I was positive he had left a hickey.

Grayson began to press his manhood through his pants against my core until we both finally climaxed. My arms were wrapped against his neck and I rested my head on his shoulder.

He held me tightly as we regained our breath.

We had just finished making out hard core and I was unaware of what to do now. It became silent as we both tried to calm ourselves down.

I always managed to push him away whenever I felt frightened of my emotions, but every time he touched me it was hard to resist. I finally realized I was just as smitten with Grayson as he was with me.

"I know you don't want to be in a relationship right now and that you would prefer if I stay away from you. But please let me stay with you for tonight Madeline. Just one night, let me have you in my arms."

I felt him tighten his hold on me. I could tell he didn't want to let me go, and if I was being completely honest right now, I didn't want him to let go of me either.

I moved back and stared into his beautiful eyes. My hands were wrapped around his neck as I held onto him.

"Fine, just for tonight."

I knew this was stupid. Just last week I had told him I didn't want anything to do with him and that I wasn't in love with him. But here I was allowing him to embrace me and kiss me as if we were dating.

Although all I wanted at this moment was to be with Grayson.

He seemed extremely happy with my answer and I felt him kiss my head.

"I love you Madeline. I love you so much that it feels like torture not to be able to kiss you and touch you. You're like a drug that I can't get enough of."

I love you too Grayson, but why can't I say it back? I hated being afraid of telling him my real feelings. Maybe I could show him how I felt rather than directly say it. It would only be for a night.

I got up and I laid under the covers while Grayson did the same. I then moved toward him as I hugged him. My head rested on his strong chest and I could hear his rapid heartbeat. It was so cute too see I made him feel this way.

He kissed my head and then began to brush my hair with his fingers.

"Remember the first day we met?"

I smiled just thinking about that day. Grayson looked so flustered.

"We were only children then but I was immediately mesmerized by your beauty. I couldn't explain why I felt butterflies whenever I saw you. No matter how hard I tried to dislike you Madeline I just couldn't."

I did remember that day. I thought Grayson hated me by how hostile he acted toward me. Although there were many times he was very kind.

"I always thought you hated me. When you told me you were in love with me back in high school, I honestly thought you were lying to me."

I was very confused about how he felt towards me then.

"I'm honestly really sorry about that. I was immature and rude. I didn't know how else to respond to these intense feelings I felt for you. By the time I found out how I truly felt about you I was afraid to tell you. After everything I had done to you I thought you hated me. I preferred having our usual arguments rather than have you hate me and push me away."

I felt like I could relate to him now. I was currently in love with him but I was too scared to admit to my feelings.

Grayson hugged me and I did the same. I loved hugging his strong body. It felt so comforting being near him.

"I'm just so happy to have you in my arms right now my love." He then kissed my head one last time.

We fell asleep in each other's arms that night. I knew I would freak out about all of this tomorrow. But for now I was enjoying every minute of it.

Sudden Trip

MADELINE POV

I woke up a bit disoriented. It took me a while to realize I wasn't in my apartment.

I sat up and it all hit me. I had made out with Grayson last night and he was supposed to be lying down next to me which he wasn't at the moment.

I was happy since I didn't feel like seeing him now after everything that had happened yesterday.

"God, why do I keep getting myself in this same mess?" I had promised myself I wouldn't be seduced by Grayson's charms.

I worried that he would be back.

Maybe I could change and get out of here. I could call Grace and tell her that I had some urgent business to attend to. Although my plans quickly vanished as I saw Grayson walk inside with a breakfast tray.

"Good morning my love. I made you some breakfast." Grayson had a bright smile on his face as he placed the tray on my side table.

He sat down on the bed and leaned in to kiss me but I panicked and moved away. I got up realizing that I shouldn't have kissed Grayson last night. Now he was acting like my boyfriend.

I turned back to look at Grayson with my arms crossed.

"Look, I know I agreed for us to be together last night but that was it. What happened between us should never have happened. You have a girlfriend for crying out loud! What we did yesterday is very unfair to her."

I had been an accomplice to his cheating last night and that wasn't the kind of person I was. I felt angry that Grayson was telling me he loves me while he was seeing someone else.

"Are you jealous?" Grayson was grinning.

"No, I just find it to be very unfair and disrespectful of me and you to be making out while you have a girlfriend."

He continued to give out that sexy laugh as he stared at me. Damn why was this man so hot?

"I'm not actually seeing her Madeline. I haven't been with anyone since you came back to New York. The girl you saw is smitten with me and said if we hung out again one last time then she would leave me alone. When she presented herself as my girlfriend I didn't deny it because I wanted to make you jealous. I know it was pitiful of me but I was desperate to see you react and admit to your feelings for me. I know you still love me Madeline, I can see it in the way you look at me and how you kissed me last night and the day you slept in my apartment."

He began to walk toward me. It felt like he was a lion trying to catch his prey. He then pulled me towards him into a gentle hug.

"Madeline, Madeline, Madeline" He repeated my name like a chant.

"You have no idea the things you make me feel whenever you're around. You make me go crazy with desire for you." He rested his head on my shoulder.

I didn't know what to do. This was all happening so fast and I didn't know if I was prepared to start a relationship with Grayson again.

"Just give me time. Whenever I think about my mother I remember the day I found out about her death. It hurt me so much that you, the man I love, had been the one keeping that secret from me for so long. I felt so stupid, so humiliated and distraught after I found out. It's hard enough for me to even be in this home with Ian and Grace."

Grayson lifted his head up and gave me a gentle kiss on my forehead.

"I can wait for as long as you need my love. If time is what you need then I will give it to you. I don't want you to feel rushed."

He grabbed my hand and kissed it.

"I'll see you downstairs. That way we can all eat together."

Grayson grabbed the tray and took it with him.

I went over to my closet and began to change. Although I couldn't help but think over everything Grayson and I spoke about.

It made me so happy to see how understanding he was being with me. I was glad he wasn't pushing me to do anything I didn't feel ready to do.

I put on some simple makeup and then grabbed my bag as I headed downstairs. I arrived at the dining room and I hugged Ian and Grace.

"Good morning my child. How did you sleep?"

I immediately thought about Grayson and I making out. Although I quickly pushed those thoughts away.

"Pretty good" I began to eat, not wanting to talk more about last night.

"I'm glad to hear that Madeline. What about you Grayson?"

Grayson stared at me as he answered.

"It was the best sleep I've had in awhile." He gave me a flirtatious wink.

Luckily Grace didn't notice.

"That's good to hear. I'm glad you two stayed over last night. I've missed you both."

We finished eating our breakfast and we said our goodbyes. I gave Grace and Ian a hug and then headed over to my car.

As I arrived at my apartment I noticed Grayson still hadn't arrived. I couldn't help but worry about him. I realized I was being over dramatic.

I loved him, more than I cared to admit. But I couldn't help but miss him whenever he wasn't around.

I entered my apartment and went over to my bathroom. I took a quick shower and I changed into some comfy clothes.

I decided it would be best to go to bed early since I was working tomorrow. I grabbed my phone to set my alarm when I noticed a text from an unknown number. As I clicked on the text I was surprised to see it was from Grayson.

"Goodnight my love. I hope we will get to see each other again tomorrow. I miss you already."

I couldn't help but smile from seeing his kind text. I decided to text him back.

"Goodnight Grayson." Is all I said. I didn't feel ready to write any heartfelt messages like he did. I was still scared about what could become of us.

I quickly drifted to sleep but I was woken up by my annoying alarm. I wasn't a morning person but my favorite ginger lemon tea helped me stay awake.

I changed into a black pencil shirt and a white button up shirt. My hair was styled down and I grabbed my work bag before heading to work.

I greeted my other coworkers and I headed over to Jack's office.

He had texted me in the morning telling me he had something important to tell me.

"Please take a seat."

We walked over to the couch and began to talk.

"Well I know this may be a surprise for you Madeline but we will be traveling to Seattle tomorrow for a business event. CEO's from different companies will all be there and it will be a great way for you to make friends and form connections with people in the business world. It will help you a lot once you inherit your grandfather's company."

He was right. This event would be excellent for me. It would surely help me once I became the CEO of my grandfather's company.

We finished our conversation and I headed to my office. I couldn't help but wonder if Grayson would be attending this event. I felt excited and happy to think that I would be seeing him again.

I finished my work early and headed back to my apartment. Jack let me out a bit early so that I could pack for tomorrow's sudden trip.

I grabbed my small suitcase and placed a couple of outfits ranging from elegant to work style clothes. We would only be staying there for two nights and we would return back to New York after that.

I finished packing and made myself some dinner. I then got ready for bed.

I grabbed my phone hoping that I would see a text from Grayson and I was pleasantly surprised. As I laid snuggled up in my bed I read his text.

"I couldn't stop thinking about you all day. I miss you so much my love. I wish you could be sleeping beside me right now and let me hold you in my arms. I hope to see you again soon. Sweet dreams Madeline."

I was internally screaming from how happy his message made me feel. He was so sweet.

"I miss you too. Sweet dreams Grayson."

I charged my phone and went back to bed. My heart was beating fast just thinking about Grayson. It was getting harder to deny my feelings for him. Every kind gesture he showed me just had me falling in love with him all over again.

The following morning I headed into a taxi and met up with Jack in his private jet.

As I entered the luxurious plane I made sure to find a spot with a window view. I placed my bag down and was about to take out a book when suddenly I heard my name being called.

"Good morning Madeline. Do you mind if I sit here?"

The voice sounded very familiar. As I looked up to see this mysterious person I was pleasantly surprised to see who it was.

Tell Me You Love Me

MADELINE POV

RECAP.......

As I entered the luxurious plane I made sure to find a spot with a window view. I placed my bag down and was about to take out a book when suddenly I heard my name being called.

"Good morning Madeline. Do you mind if I sit here?"

The voice sounded very familiar. As I looked up to see this mysterious person I was pleasantly surprised to see who it was.

END OF RECAP...

"It's fine, go ahead." Grayson smiled and sat on the seat in front of me.

I was happy he was here and sitting so close to me.

I tried to read my book but I couldn't. I could feel Grayson's hard stare and I suddenly felt a bit shy.

I closed my book and looked at him.

"What is it?" I asked curiously.

"I'll tell you everything you want to know if you sit next to me." He gave me a wink as he finished.

He was smart. I knew he wanted to get my attention so that I could sit beside him. I decided to play this game of his. I honestly didn't mind being closer to him.

Maybe I would try this out. I wanted Grayson just as much as he wanted me. There was no harm in me sitting next to him.

"Alright then" I said.

He was grinning and I realized my answer made him happy.

I walked over to the other side and sat beside him. He immediately wrapped his arm around my waist and pulled me closer to him.

I then felt him whisper something in my ear.

"You're so beautiful Madeline. I can't seem to take my eyes off you." He kissed my cheek and moved lower to my neck.

His gentle kisses and caress felt so good. I didn't want him to stop. I closed my eyes enjoying the way he touched my body.

"You have to stop. Someone might see us." I was whispering.

Jack was too busy on his phone with his wife to notice what was happening with Grayson and I.

Grayson stopped kissing me but didn't let go of me. I laid my head on his shoulder and closed my eyes.

"I love you Madeline." I heard him say before kissing my head.

I slept throughout the whole plane ride. I always felt the most comfortable sleeping beside Grayson. He had always made me feel safer.

It wasn't until Grayson woke me up that I realized we had arrived in Seattle.

"Wake up my love, we've arrived in Seattle."

I woke up to see a handsome Grayson smiling at me. He gently brushed my hair.

I felt a bit shy for having slept throughout the whole plane ride. I wonder if I bothered him in my sleep?

I moved out of my seat and I grabbed my luggage. Jack and Grayson grabbed their suitcases and we all headed out toward the limousine that was waiting for us outside.

Before we knew it we were all in our hotel rooms. The business party would be held tonight so I decided to start getting ready now. I always preferred to be ready a bit earlier.

I curled my hair and I did my makeup. I then changed into a well fitted black dress I had specially picked out for today. As soon as I was done I headed downstairs to the lobby to meet up with Grayson and Jack. We were going to a limousine and going to the event from there.

I decided to sit down in one of the chairs as I waited for Jack and Grayson to arrive. Although before I could sit, I felt someone tap my shoulder.

"Excuse me beautiful, are you here alone?" It was a handsome man who was clearly flirting with me.

I was about to turn him down when I heard Grayson's voice.

"She's mine. So move along." Grayson wrapped a possessive arm around my waist as he stared at the man who had just tried to talk to me.

The other guy gave up pretty fast and left. Watching Grayson act like that was pretty hot but I hated the idea of being owned.

"Thank you but I could've handled that on my own."

I attempted to move away from Grayson but he held me in place.

He gently brushed my hair back and whispered in my ear.

"I hate seeing other men after you. It makes me burn with jealousy."

He then faced me and kissed the side of my lips. I wanted him to kiss me, to press his lips against mine, but he didn't. He preferred to tease me.

"You're mine Madeline." He said before moving apart from me.

Jack had finally arrived and we all headed over to the limousine. Grayson sat next to me and I couldn't help but notice how close our bodies were from each other. He would occasionally press his leg against mine. Which I didn't really mind.

I made eye contact with him as I observed his handsome face. I would much prefer to be going out on a date with Grayson than to go to this event. But I knew this was important. I couldn't let my emotions get the best of me.

Finally we had arrived. I headed inside the building with Grayson and Jack. The building was very grand and there were a lot of people. Luckily Grayson and Jack knew most of the individuals here already so they introduced me to their business associates.

We talked and conversed about our companies. I formed connections with other business people and I knew this would help me in the future.

Soon the event ended and we headed back to the hotel. It was already 10 pm and I felt exhausted from the trip and the party.

"How about we go out to eat? We haven't had dinner and I can't go to bed with an empty stomach."

"I'll pass, I'm exhausted. I just want to sleep. I'll see you two tomorrow." I answered.

"Good night Madeline, I'll see you tomorrow." Jack smiled.

I turned around to head over to my room but Grayson caught up to me.

"Can we talk?"

"I'll wait for you downstairs." Jack said to Grayson before heading to the elevator.

It was just Grayson and I.

"Would you like to enter my room?"

"Sure"

It was 10 pm and people were probably sleeping at this hour. It was best that we talk in his room.

He opened the door and led me inside. I didn't plan to be here for long. Whenever I was alone with Grayson I couldn't think straight.

I turned around to face him. He looked like he wanted to touch me but he held back. His hands were formed in tight fists as if he waa trying to control himself. I wondered if he wanted to kiss me.

"Madeline I can't keep doing this. I promised you that I would never force you to do anything you don't feel comfortable doing, and I plan on keeping that promise. But I need to know how you truly feel about me. Everytime I see you I have to force myself not to touch you."

He ran his fingers through his hair. I could see the desperation in his eyes. He was clearly holding back from touching me right now.

"Everytime you're near me I have to fight the urge not to pull you against me and kiss you."

He moved closer to me, our lips were almost touching. I could feel his body heat. Grayson looked into my eyes almost asking for permission.

"Just tell me you love me Madeline. That's all I need to hear from you." He spoke in such a low voice it was almost a whisper.

I stared back into his, wanting to say something. I wanted to kiss him so bad but I was terrified. Getting back with Grayson frightened me.

I loved him so much I didn't want to lose him like I lost my mother. He had also lied to me in the past.

I pushed him away and left the room. I wouldn't realize the mistake I had just commited until it was too late. I was being a coward but it felt safe in the moment.

I Love Him

MADELINE POV

I entered my hotel room and began to cry. I was so stupid and a coward for having left Grayson. I didn't even dare look at his face.

"I should have just been honest." I told myself.

I took off my clothes and got into the shower. After another good cry I headed out and put on my sleepwear. I laid on the bed and began to read a book I had brought with me. After an hour or so I stopped. It was almost 2 in the morning so I decided to sleep.

I put my book on the side table when suddenly my phone began to ring. I was surprised to see it was Jack.

"Hello"

"Sorry for bothering you Madeline. It's just that Grayson and I are at a bar right now and he's gotten so drunk. He's been talking about you nonstop and he won't stop drinking. I need you to help me get him out of here. You're the only one he will listen to."

I could hear the concern in his voice.

"It's alright. I'll be right there." I tried to calm him down.

"I'll send you the address right away."

"Thank you Jack." I hung up and quickly changed.

I grabbed my bag and headed out.

I took a taxi to their location and finally I had arrived at the bar.

After going through security I finally saw Grayson and Jack sitting at the bar. I quickly ran over to them.

Grayson had his head down while Jack patted his back.

"What's wrong?" I asked Jack.

"Thank god you're here." He seemed relieved I had finally arrived.

"Please talk to him. He won't listen to me."

I nodded as my way of telling him I would handle this.

"Grayson, it's me Madeline. Let's go back to the hotel. You've been drinking too much already." I tried to speak in the most gentle way possible.

I touched his elbow to get his attention.

He immediately looked up and I saw tears running down his cheeks. It broke my heart seeing him like that.

"Why should I go with you? You don't love me."

He was pouting and being extremely vulnerable at this moment. This confirmed my suspicions that he was drunk.

I immediately wrapped my arms around his large frame. He hugged me back as I felt his arms around my waist.

"Please Grayson, let's go back to the hotel. " I whispered in his ear.

I moved back and began to wipe away his tears with my sleeve. I gave him a kiss on the cheek and I grabbed his hand. He didn't push away and simply followed me.

"Thank you." Jack said.

I smiled at him in return.

Luckily the taxi was still waiting for me outside so I helped Grayson inside. Jack came with us as as well.

As soon as we arrived I opened the door for my room and let Grayson walk in. I prefered that he stay in my room instead. He was still drunk and I wanted to take care of him.

I helped him get to my bed and he laid down. I took off his shoes and helped him take off his blazer. He seemed tired so I decided to leave him alone.

I tried to walk away but I felt Grayson grab my hand.

"Please don't leave me. I love you Madeline."

I stopped and went over to him. I laid on the opposite side of the bed. He immediately cuddled up next to me.

"Why are you hurting me Madeline? I love you so much but you always push me away. I know you love me but you're just too scared to admit it. I promise to take care of you and love you always. All I want is you Madeline, why can't you understand that?"

Tears began to fall down his cheeks. I could see he was in pain. All this time I had been so scared to admit to my real feelings for Grayson. I worried he could hurt me again but in the end I've been the one hurting him. I've led him on and then pushed him away.

I began to cry, I hated seeing him like this. I never wanted him to be in so much pain. I hugged him, craving his warmth. He did the same.

I began to gently brush his hair. He seemed to enjoy it.

"Grayson I'm so sorry for hurting you. I've been a coward and you're right. I'm too scared to admit to my feelings. But I think I know now, well I think I've always known that you would take care of me. I know that you never wanted to see me in pain so that's why you kept my mom's death a secret from me. I've finally come to terms with it all."

I knew it was time for me to say it.

"I love you Grayson."

It felt amazing to finally admit to my feelings. Especially since I was saying it out loud to the person who needed to hear it the most.

I looked at Grayson and realized he was asleep. He didn't hear my confession nor anything else I had said to him.

I would have to wait until tomorrow morning to say it to him. I was happy that at least I had finally made the decision to tell Grayson I love him.

I kissed Grayson's head and we slept next to each other the whole night.

Whenever I was with Grayson I felt so at peace. The following morning came soon and I woke up extremely excited to tell Grayson I love him.

I looked to my side but Grayson wasn't there. I immediately stood up to look for him around the room but he was nowhere to be found.

I changed and did my makeup. I was supposed to meet up with Jack and Grayson this morning so we could go eat breakfast together. We still had one more day in Seattle and we planned to explore the city.

Although I wondered where Grayson could be.

I knocked on Grayson's door but he wouldn't respond. I then went over to Jack's room to see if he knew about Grayson's whereabouts.

Jack immediately opened the door.

"I was just about to go to your room. Did something happen between you and Grayson?"

Jack looked concerned and that worried me.

"Why? Is something wrong with Grayson? He left my hotel room without leaving a note. I checked his room but he didn't answer."

I just wanted to find Grayson.

"He left for the airport early in the morning, he's flying back to New York today. In fact he's probably already home."

I was shocked.

"What do you mean he left? I really need to talk to him! We have to go back to New York Jack. I need to see him." I felt desperate to go to him.

He didn't know I confessed to him last night. All he remembered was me rejecting him. He must be feeling so distraught right now. I wanted to see him. I wanted to embrace him and tell him I love him.

I felt so mad and angry with myself. I should have been honest with my feelings since the beginning. Now I was facing the consequences of my actions.

"I don't know what happened with you two last night but he looked pretty bad after you two talked. He wouldn't stop drinking either. I'm glad you went to get him yesterday at the bar, but he looked even worse this morning when he called. I could hear it in his voice, he seemed upset. It didn't sound like him."

What did I do! I was the one hurting him. He had only been sweet and understanding with me the whole time. He had worked so hard to win me back. Now it was my turn to chase after him and tell him how I truly felt.

I Love You Grayson

MADELINE POV

I was currently in a limousine waiting to be dropped off at my apartment. I couldn't wait to see Grayson. Although I couldn't help but worry that he could be upset or maybe angry with me for rejecting him so many times yet leading him on.

"You're nervous, aren't you." Jack held my hand to comfort me.

"It's going to be ok. Grayson is madly in love with you and has been since you two were children. He will accept your confession, so don't worry so much. I know my brother, he'll be happy once he finds out how you truly feel about him."

I had told Jack about everything that had been going on between Grayson and I. He carefully listened to what I had to say and even gave me some advice. He had always been a supportive brother figure.

"Thank you Jack." I gave him a weak smile.

Finally I had arrived at my apartment. I grabbed my luggage and said goodbye to Jack.

"Say hello to Kennedy for me."

"Of course! I'll see you, bye!"

I walked towards the entrance of the building and then headed to the elevator. As soon as I entered my apartment I left my suitcase and headed out to talk with Grayson.

I knocked on his door but he wouldn't answer. I wondered if he was home or if he was just ignoring me.

The elevator doors suddenly opened up and I turned back to see my biggest nightmare.

Grayson and his past hookup Emily had just gotten out of the elevator together. Emily was clinging onto him which irritated the hell out of me.

It felt like someone had just punched me in the stomach just seeing them together like that. But I wasn't going to give up so easily. He needed to know how I truly felt about him.

As they walked toward his apartment they stopped and then looked at me.

"Can we talk?"

"Can't you see we're together? Just leave us alone." Emily then rolled her eyes in annoyance.

This woman was extremely rude. You could tell she was arrogant. Why would Grayson go out with someone like her?

"I wasn't talking to you." I responded.

I stared at Grayson hoping he would agree. He simply looked at me with such sad eyes. He looked like a lost puppy.

"I'm sorry, I don't feel like talking right now."

Those words broke my heart. He needed to know how I felt about him. I just wanted to run and kiss him.

I had clearly hurt him and now he was pushing me away.

He moved around me and walked inside his apartment with Emily.

I felt like crying. He had never tried to avoid me or push me away before. I wondered if this is how he felt when I had told him I didn't want him near me.

I went inside my apartment and began to cry. No matter what I would find the way to talk to him. But for now I couldn't contain this pain I felt and I continued to cry. It felt like I had just gone through a breakup.

The following day I was even more determined to win Grayson back. I wore a sexy yet elegant outfit. I was going to work today but after that I would go and talk to Grayson.

I wanted to look my best for when I would see him. My hair was styled down since I knew Grayson loved when my hair was styled this way.

As soon as I got to work I couldn't stop thinking about how I would confess to Grayson. Would he accept me? Maybe he hated me now. I was beginning to feel discouraged.

I finished work early and went back to my apartment to leave my work bag and retouch up my makeup and hair. I was beginning to worry about how I looked and if the words would come out alright.

As soon as I knocked on the door my heart began to beat fast. I felt excited yet scared at the same time. I really hoped he would accept my confession and that we would finally be together.

He opened the door and as soon as I saw his handsome face I felt so much better. All of my worries just vanished and I felt this sense of confidence.

I loved this man, I have always loved this man and nothing and no one was going to separate me from him.

"Can we talk?"

He looked surprised. I wondered if he thought I had given up on speaking to him.

"Alright, come in."

He seemed distant. He wasn't the happy and positive Grayson I knew him to be.

He opened the door for me and we walked toward his living room. We sat down on his couch and he waited for me to speak.

"I wanted to apologize to you for what happened in Seattle. I should have never left the room when you were opening up to me. It was rude of me and I genuinely feel awful for it. I've also led you on and pushed you away multiple times, and for that I'm also terribly sorry. My intention was never to hurt you Grayson. I was just scared that if we were together again I would end up the one hurt like what happened on the day of our graduation."

I felt tears falling down my cheeks but I was able to keep my composure.

I noticed Grayson become upset. I knew he hated seeing me cry.

I wiped away my tears and continued to speak.

"My father wasn't a good example of what a man should treat those he loves. It was a short time that I lived with him but what he did to my mother and I is something I can never forget. All of it just haunts me to this day. But once I got to know you and your family, my whole world changed. My mother always cared for me but unfortunately she wasn't there for most of my life. Although what she did give me was a new family. I love your family Grayson. Your mom and dad raised me and it honestly feels like they're also my parents. Your brother is amazing and I see him like the older brother I always wanted. But with you Grayson, you've been my friend and companion my whole life. You teased me when we were kids and cared for me when we were teenagers. When we began to date back in high school I was also scared to be romantically involved with you but every gentle touch, sweet kiss, and the love you showed me made me change my idea of what a man was. You aren't my father and you will never be him. I'm so happy to have you in my life."

I was finally going to say it. After years of being apart and pushing him away it was finally time for me to admit to my feelings.

"I love you Grayson. I've never stopped loving you."

I sat there trying to figure out what Grayson could be thinking. Would he reject me?

He stared at me in bewilderment. A couple of minutes went by and he still wouldn't respond. I wonder if he was thinking at the moment.

I stood up getting ready to leave. He clearly looked uncomfortable. He was probably going to reject me.

"I'm sorry, I can see you're uncomfortable. I think it's best if I leave." I was running away again. But I couldn't take the idea of being rejected by the man I love.

As I began to walk away he quickly grabbed my hand. He stood up and I stared back at him.

[WARNING MATURE CONTENT]

He pulled me against him. His strong arms were wrapped around my waist and then I felt his lips press against mine.

I immediately wrapped my arms around his neck trying to deepen the kiss. Grayson's hands roamed around my body until he settled on my ass.

He gave them a light squeeze and then began to massage them.

My body began to feel hot.

We tilted our heads side to side as we kissed passionately. I truly wanted this man. He ignited a fire within me whenever he touched me.

He then took off my dress and proceeded to kiss me. I was semi naked with only my undergarments on. Although Grayson didn't seem to mind.

He moved backward and sat on the couch. I sat on top of him and we continued to kiss.

I felt Grayson's hands back on my ass and he began to press his manhood against my core.

I began to moan from the pleasure he was giving me. I felt his lips on my neck as he began to carefully place kisses on my bare skin. I tilted my head to give him more acces.

"You're so beautiful. I can never get enough of you Madeline."

He took off my bra exposing my breast. I felt him begin to lick and suck on my sensitive chest. I tried to contain my moans but everywhere he touched me felt hot.

"Don't cover your mouth, I love hearing your voice when I pleasure you."

He continued to touch me. Every kiss and gentle touch was intoxicating. It was as if admitting to him that I love him ignited this passion between us both.

I then felt him move upward toward my lips and once again we kissed. He began to take off his shirt and I helped him out. His exposed six pack was hot and my hands roamed around his body.

He took off the rest of his clothes and I did the same. Now we were both naked. I sat on top of him as we continued to kiss.

He grabbed my ass and pressed his manhood against my entrance. I moved at his rhythm moving up and down on top of him. It felt amazing.

I began to moan again from how good he made me feel.

Grayson began to kiss my neck again and began to suck on it. I was definitely going to get a hickey from this.

As soon as we felt the pleasure consume us we reached our climax.

We headed over to Grayson's shower and began to make out. There was this strong attraction I felt for Grayson that simply couldn't be satisfied.

He picked me up and pressed his manhood inside me once again.

"I love you so much Madeline." He whispered before kissing me.

He began to move in and out of me at a faster speed making me go wild. I couldn't contain my moans

Finally we both reached our climax and we showered.

As soon as I got out Grayson handed me a towel. I dried my body and wrapped the towel around me. Grayson had his around his bottom half exposing his sexy six pack.

I didn't realize I had been staring at him so long because he suddenly noticed and began to tease me for it.

"You want to go at it again princess? I can go for round three." Grayson winked at me, making me blush.

I turned around trying not to look at his handsome face. I suddenly felt shy. We had just made love not too long ago and that sudden boldness of mine had now vanished.

[END OF MATURE CONTENT]

Grayson grabbed some boxers and a T-shirt from his drawer and handed them to me.

"Here, wear this." He said to me.

"You know I live next door Grayson. I can go to my apartment and grab a change of clothes."

Grayson pulled me toward him as his arms wrapped around my waist.

"I like seeing you in my clothes."

I wondered if he had fantasized of me wearing his t-shirt and boxers. I guess it would be fine, I liked smelling like Grayson. His scent was phenomenal.

"Very well then." I smiled.

I put on the items he gave me and he changed into a T-shirt and pajama pants.

He grabbed my hand and led me to the living room. We decided to order takeout since we didn't feel like cooking.

I sat next to Grayson as I faced him.

He grabbed my hands and kissed them.

We were finally going to talk about my confession and how that made Grayson feel. I really wanted to know why he was with Emily and why he had left back home to New York so early.

"You have no idea how happy hearing your confession made me feel. Hearing you say you love me made me feel like the happiest man alive. I know I messed up in the past but I I want you to know that I will take care of you and make sure I never hurt you again."

This man was so sweet, I was so happy that finally we would be together.

"I will be honest, I was distraught and sad last night when you left me. I had hoped that you would confess to me yesterday but when you denied your feelings once again I just couldn't take it anymore. I need to know your mine, I need to know that you love me, and I desperately need to be able to touch you and kiss you for me to be around you. It was becoming too painful not being able to be with you. That's why I got drunk yesterday, I didn't know what else I could do to forget about you."

I felt terrible for having him go through something like that. My intention was never to hurt the man I love.

"When you told me you wanted to talk, I assumed you were going to reject me. So I got scared and decided to avoid you. But when you came back today and showed up at my door I just couldn't push you away. I can't seem to be away from you for too long."

I felt the exact same way. Grayson was all I could think about from the moment I moved back to New York. Although if I was being completely honest, I had never forgotten about him. I had always wondered what would have happened between us if I had never left with my grandparents.

Although something tells me would have still been together. Grayson was the only man I saw myself with for the rest of my life.

Grayson moved closer to me and he gave me a gentle kiss on my lips. I closed my eyes savoring the sweet moment.

We stopped and I proceeded to ask Grayson a question I was dying to know the answer to.

"Why were you with Emily?"

I didn't like that woman. It made me jealous just thinking about her touching Grayson. Wait, when had I become so possessive over Grayson?

I saw Grayson smirk and I knew he was about to tease me again.

"Is my princess jealous?" He asked teasingly.

"Maybe" I answered.

He began to laugh. He showed his teeth showcasing his charming smile. This man was extremely handsome. Well the whole Lockwood family was attractive. Even at an older age Ian and Grace looked amazing. Jack was equally as attractive as Grayson, although in my opinion Grayson was far more handsome.

"You don't have to worry my love. Her father is a business man and I ended up going back to New York with him. Emily and her mom picked us up from the airport and we all went to have lunch after that. When they were taking me back home she decided to walk with me to my apartment. I was really bummed out about what had happened between us and she noticed my behavior. I didn't tell her how I was feeling and told her I was ok but she insisted on dropping me off at my apartment. I gave up and allowed her to do it. When I saw you and I told you to leave me alone I felt like such an asshole. Emily entered my apartment but I practically kicked her as soon as she got inside. I didn't want anyone with me that wasn't you. You are all I can think about Madeline."

Hearing him say that made me feel so relieved.

I smiled at him.

"Well in that case, I'm no longer feeling jealous because you're mine now."

Grayson seemed to like the idea.

"I like the sound of that. I'm all yours my love like all of you belongs to me."

I moved closer toward Grayson and I rested my head on his chest as we snuggled up together on the couch.

I felt Grayson kiss my head as he began to brush my hair.

"Tell me you love me one more time. I love hearing you say it."

He was so cute.

"I love you Grayson. I've always loved you."

Grayson wrapped his strong arms around me encasings me in a warm hug.

This moment was perfect. I couldn't understand why I had deprived myself from this feeling. Grayson was all I ever wanted. I just hoped no one would mess this up, including myself.

Let's go to Paris!

M ADELINE POV

RECAP

I moved closer toward Grayson and I rested my head on his chest as we snuggled up together on the couch.

I felt Grayson kiss my head as he began to brush my hair.

"Tell me you love me one more time. I love hearing you say it."

He was so cute.

"I love you Grayson. I've always loved you."

Grayson wrapped his strong arms around me encasings me in a warm hug.

This moment was perfect. I couldn't understand why I had deprived myself from this feeling. Grayson was all I ever wanted. I just hoped no one would mess this up, including myself.

END OF RECAP

The doorbell rang and our food came. We decided to watch a movie while we ate our dinner.

"How about we watch ratatouille?" I asked Grayson. It was my favorite film.

"Sounds good to me." He answered with a smile.

We sat next to each other and began to watch the film as we ate. After we finished eating I snuggled up next to Grayson again.

It was getting late and I began to feel tired. I closed my eyes feeling the warmth and comfort of being in Grayson's arms. He carefully held me close to him until I fell asleep.

GRAYSON POV

The movie was almost over. I looked over at Madeline and I realized my beautiful princess had fallen asleep. I turned off the TV and carefully picked her up. I didn't want to wake her up.

I then placed her on my bed and put a blanket over her. I moved to the other side and I pulled her against me wanting to have her close to me.

I was so happy that I could finally be close to the woman I love. She was so beautiful and strong. I was aware of the pain she suffered as a child and how much I had hurt her by keeping such a big secret from her.

I just wanted to protect her and care for her now. I wanted to be by her side at all times. Madeline was all I could think about day and night. It made me feel like the happiest man alive to hear her say she loves me.

Just being able to touch her and have her in my arms revives me. I can't seem to be away from her for too long. Just looking at her brightens my day. She's my whole world. I love her so much and I will do everything in power to make sure she's happy.

I turned off the lights and I fell asleep next to my princess.

MADELINE POV

I woke up and was sad to see that Grayson wasn't lying down beside me. I remembered all of the events from yesterday. I couldn't help but feel shy for what Grayson and I had done. We had made love twice. Although I was happy that we would finally be together.

I got up and went straight to the bathroom. I threw some water on my face and I grabbed some mouthwash since I didn't have a tooth brush. All of my things were back in my apartment.

I brushed my hair and I walked out to look for Grayson. I wanted to see him. It was weird but I missed him already. I guess I was truly in love with him, he was all I could think about.

As I arrived at the kitchen I saw Grayson placing some food on a tray. There were pancakes with syrup and a bowl of fruit. I wonder if he had planned to surprise me with breakfast in bed?

He looked up at me and smiled. He was still wearing his sleepwear but he still looked crazy handsome. His beautiful hazel eyes stared into mine.

"I was planning to surprise you with breakfast in bed but I guess I was too late."

I walked over to him and embraced him. His arms wrapped around my waist as he held onto me. It felt good having his strong and warm body against mine. I felt him kiss my head.

"Good morning Grayson. Thank you for the lovely breakfast but now that I'm awake, why don't we eat breakfast here at the table."

He looked at me and gave me a gentle kiss on the lips.

"I would love that."

We sat at the table and we ate breakfast together. I had work today so after we ate I headed over to my apartment and changed.

Grayson was going to take me to work so I met him at the elevator.

As I walked out of my apartment I saw a handsome Grayson wearing a suit. This was his usual work attire but I always found it attractive when he wore one. Who am I kidding, he looked hot in everything he wore.

He walked to me and grabbed my hand.

"You look beautiful my love." He said as he kissed my hand.

"You look handsome in that suit."

"Of course I do. I look good in everything." He said teasingly.

He was very conceited. He knew he was hot and extremely attractive.

"That may be true but you also look great wearing nothing." I decided to tease him as well.

I walked into the elevator and he quickly followed.

As soon as the doors closed he began to kiss me. Although it wasn't a sweet peck on the lips but instead a hungry, passionate kiss.

I wrapped my arms around his neck while his possessively held my waist. I closed my eyes, savoring the moment. Grayson was an excellent kisser. He put his tongue in and it turned into a sensual kiss.

I began to feel Grayson's hands move down to my ass. He gave them a tight squeeze and then began to massage them. I then felt him begin to press himself against my core through his clothes.

I could tell Grayson was turned on.

I could feel his hard on pressing against me. We really needed to stop before someone saw us.

As soon as the elevator doors opened he stopped.

"Don't tease me like that baby, I won't be able to stop next time."

My body felt hot. This man was way too good at this. I tried to calm myself down but I couldn't forget the moment we had just shared.

Grayson opened the car door for me to enter and I got in. He went around and then turned on the car. The car ride was silent.

I guess we were both trying hard not to think about our little make out session in the elevator. We were lucky no one saw us. We had finally arrived at my workplace.

"Let's eat lunch together. I'll pick you up when you're ready."

I gave Grayson a quick peck on the lips.

"I would love that. I'll send you a text when I'm ready." I waved goodbye and I entered the building. When I got into my office I couldn't help but feel excited to see Grayson later.

I already missed him even though he had just dropped me off.

I decided to focus on my work and get some things done. Luckily I was able to concentrate. Being with Grayson made me so happy I felt almost revived. I loved my job but somehow things just seemed even better now.

Before I knew it, it was time for my lunch break. I texted Grayson and he picked me up. We then headed to a French restaurant.

Apparently Grayson had made a reservation so we were quickly taken to our table. Grayson pulled out a chair for me to sit down. He had always been a gentleman.

"Thank you" I said to him.

We quickly ordered and as soon as the waiter left Grayson grabbed my hands and kissed them.

"I'm so happy we're finally together. Being able to take you out for lunch like this feels amazing. I can see you whenever I want and I can finally touch you. Touching you had been almost like a drug that I tried to stay away from. I had deprived myself of that selfish desire in order not to hurt you."

I felt bad for pushing him away so much. Grayson was a good man. He had always tried to be careful in order not to hurt me. He accepted my boundaries and didn't pressure me into doing something I didn't feel comfortable or ready to do.

"But ever since you told me you love me I've been so happy. I thought that once you were finally with me this urge to see you and have you by my side at all times would subside. But I couldn't be any more wrong. It appears I only desire you more my love."

I could see how genuine he was. The way he looked at me were the eyes of a man in love.

"Well you don't have to worry anymore because I'll always be yours. I love you Grayson, I have never stopped loving you."

Grayson smiled at me, clearly happy with my response.

Our food came and we began to eat.

"I know this may be sudden but I booked us some tickets to France next week. I know you've always wanted to go to Paris."

I looked over at Grayson in surprise. It was quite sudden but the idea of being in Paris with Grayson made me super happy.

"This is quite sudden but I wouldn't want anything more than to visit the city of love with you."

I knew my response was cringy but I couldn't help it. I was in love with the man.

"I couldn't agree more."

Although he didn't seem to mind.

"I'll have to talk with Jack about the trip. I'm not sure if I can go."

I didn't think Jack would mind. I was ahead of schedule since I was excellent at my job. I was almost done with one of our projects. I still had enough time to get a lot of work done from now until the trip.

"You don't have to worry about that my love. I already talked with Jack about it. He said it's completely fine."

I guess Grayson had really planned this out well.

"Wow, you really planned this out well."

I could see he was eager to spend more time with me. This trip would be a good time for us to catch up and spend more time together as a couple.

My lunch break was over and Grayson took me back to my workplace.

I worked even harder on the project and since I wanted it to be finished before I left for Paris. I hadn't realized the time, my shift was over.

I texted Grayson I was off work now and he said he was on his way. While I waited for him to arrive, I took the time to talk to Jack.

I headed over to his office and we began to talk about the trip.

"I just wanted to thank you for letting me go on a trip on such short notice. I promise the project will be done before then"

"You have nothing to worry about Madeline. I'm really happy you and Grayson are taking this trip together. When he called me he seemed really excited about it."

Grayson was so cute. He was so sweet and I could see how much he truly cared about me.

"I honestly haven't seen Grayson that happy in a long time. Well not since you too were dating back in high school. After you left he changed so much. He was distant and serious all the time. My parents and I rarely saw him. But ever since you came back to New York he's becoming the same cheerful Grayson he was before. It's all thanks to you Madeline. And now that you've confessed to him he's a much happier person. He adores you Madeline, you're all he ever talks about."

It broke my heart to hear how much he had changed because of me. I knew it hurt him to see me leave him. But I was happy we had gotten over all of that.

"I'm honestly much happier now. Even though I left him I still never stopped thinking about him. Now that I'm back in New York and I've spent time with Grayson once again, I'm positive that he's the only person I want to spend the rest of my life with. I love him Jack."

I got a text message and I realized Grayson was already here.

"I have to go. Grayson is here."

"Have a good night." I was about to go but I heard Jack call my name.

"Wait! Madeline I almost forgot. My mom wants us all to have dinner tomorrow. Please make sure to tell Grayson."

I missed Grace and Ian.

"Of course we'll come. Have a good night."

"You too Madeline."

I hugged Jack goodbye and I met up with Grayson. I entered his car and I told him that Grace wanted to have dinner with us all.

"Of course we're coming. It's been a while since we've visited the place."

Grayson held my hand while he used his other one to drive. I found it endearing how he always needed to hold my hand.

We got out of his car and entered the elevator. As soon as we got out I headed over to my apartment to grab some of my stuff. I grabbed a pair of clothes and my daily essentials. I then headed over to Grayson's apartment.

As soon as I got in I put my bags in Grayson's bedroom. I had already changed into some comfortable clothing like Grayson did. We were probably going to watch a movie together.

I headed over to the kitchen and I helped Grayson make dinner. As soon as the food was ready we sat down in the dining room and we began to eat.

I felt Grayson grab my hand.

"I was thinking, you should move in with me."

I would have been scared to move in with him before, but now it just felt right. I had lived with him before. I love him and if this meant I could spend more time with him then I would take that chance.

"I love that idea. If it means I can spend more time with you then I will do it." I answered.

He kissed my hands.

We walked over to the living room and we decided to watch a movie. I snuggled up next to Grayson as he wrapped his arms around me.

I felt safe and comfortable being with him. I ended up falling asleep. The last thing I remember was feeling the soft bed and a warm blanket while hearing Grayson whisper.

"I love you Madeline."

Jealousy

MADELINE POV

We had arrived at Grace and Ian's home. I rang the doorbell and a maid opened the door to greet us.

"They're in the dining room." She said to us.

"Thank you" I answered.

Grayson held my hand as we walked over to the dining room

As soon as we arrived, we greeted everyone.

Jack and his wife Kennedy were already here.

"It's so nice to have all my kids here with me. It's been a while since we had dinner together." Grace was clearly happy.

I had missed Grace and Ian. They were like my parents.

"So what's the big surprise?" Jack asked.

I was also curious.

"He was supposed to be here already. I wonder what's taking him so long?" Grace spoke.

I wonder who she was talking about?

Suddenly I saw William walk in.

"William just moved to New York. He found a job at a hospital here so I thought we could celebrate with him." Grace seemed very proud of him.

I stood up and hugged William.

It had been a while since I had last seen him. He was like a brother to me and my best friend when I was living in England.

"It's nice to see you William. Congratulations on your new job."

"Thank you. It's nice to see you too Madeline." He smiled.

Jack also got up and hugged him.

"Congratulations William." He said.

Grayson on the other hand stayed seated and simply told Jack congrats.

I went back to my seat next to Grayson.

Grace had made us lasagna so we all began to eat.

"So when did you arrive in New York?" Jack asked.

"Last week. I wanted to settle into my new apartment before seeing you all. It's been nice so far, I really like the city."

"I'm glad." Jack answered.

"If you need a tour guide I'm happy to show you some cool spots. After all, you did the same for me when I was living in London."

William had been extremely helpful in making the transition from New York to London much easier. He was well acquainted with the city and he took me to some nice places. I was in a dark place in my life at that time and he helped me get through it. I wanted to thank him somehow.

"Thank you Madeline. I would love that." He smiled.

I felt a hand on my thigh. I turned toward Grayson and I noticed he looked serious. I realized he was irritated. It was probably because of William.

Grayson was aware that William had feelings for me. But I was sure that William no longer felt that way about me. I had rejected him and told him that I only saw him as a friend. I'm sure he was over me by now and had a girlfriend.

I felt Grayson begin to caress my thigh as he moved higher toward my core. I tried to remove his hand but he was way too strong. He pressed a finger against my sensitive core and it was then that I panicked.

I quickly grabbed his hand before he could go any further.

Grayson was upset and he was making sure I was aware of his feelings.

I held his hand and kissed it. Luckily it helped him calm down a bit.

GRAYSON POV

As soon as I heard the news that William was moving to New York I felt worried. He had spent time with Madeline for so long when we weren't together. He had her all to himself when I couldn't be with her. I couldn't help but worry that she might have romantic feelings toward him.

When she saw him she immediately ran and hugged him. I hated how William had embraced Madeline. Seeing her in his arms just irritated me. I was aware they were friends but William didn't see her simply as a friend. He was clearly in love with her.

The way he looked into her eyes when she spoke or when he simply looked at her made it obvious he liked her.

They had this connection and shared a past that I wasn't a part of. It scared me to think that she might grow romantic feelings for him now that he was here in New York. It irritated me seeing her be so kind and attentive with him.

Madeline was mine. I wanted the whole world to know it. No man was allowed to touch her except me, and William needed to know that.

MADELINE POV

After we finished eating we all said our goodbyes. I hugged everyone, including William. I had a feeling that Grayson felt jealous of my friendship with William, but there was nothing romantic between us. He was a good friend of mine and I wasn't going to be rude and ignore him simply because Grayson didn't want me to get close to William.

We got inside the car and Grayson began to drive.

He wouldn't speak to me and held a firm grasp on the wheel. I could see he was tense.

Finally we had arrived at our apartment. I couldn't take this tension anymore so I asked Grayson what was wrong.

"Are you ok? You've been silent since the car ride."

I could tell Grayson was upset. I just wanted him to talk to me about how he was feeling.

"You were all over him."

He finally spoke. He seemed furious.

"What are you talking about?" I was only being kind to William. In no way was I all over him.

"I am talking about William. As soon as you saw him you practically clung onto him. And then you asked him out right in front of me. I know William is in love with you, I can see it in the way he looks at you."

"William is not in love with me. I didn't cling onto him, I just gave him a hug like everyone else at the gathering. And he doesn't look at me with loving eyes."

Grayson was clearly jealous.

"He does, I would know because I recognize that look too well. It's the same way I look at you every day."

I didn't see it that way but I understood why he viewed it differently. I thought of William as a dear friend but that was it. I didn't love him in that way. Grayson was the only man that made my heart skip a beat or made me feel immensely happy just by being near him. But if I put myself in his shoes and saw him be that attentive toward Emily then I would be just as jealous.

I grabbed Grayson's hand and kissed it.

"I didn't mean to hurt your feelings. I was just excited to see William since he's a good friend of mine. But I don't have any romantic feelings towards him and I never have. I'm in love with you Grayson. It has always been that way since we first started dating back in high school."

Grayson seemed to have calmed down a bit.

I moved closer to him and I began to caress his left cheek. He closed his eyes, clearly enjoying the moment.

He placed his left hand over mine and he opened his eyes.

"I love you Grayson. I'm yours. My heart, soul, and body belong to you. Just like you belong to me. I don't want you to feel threatened by William. The only person I want is you."

I placed my hands on the sides of his face as I pulled him in for a kiss. His hand shifted down to my waist as he wrapped his arms around me.

[MATURE CONTENT AHEAD]

My arms were wrapped around his neck as the kiss changed from a simple peck to a passionate make out.

I felt him pick me up and he sat me on the table. He began to take off my shirt leaving me simply in my bra. We continued to kiss as we held each other close. He began to lick and suck on my neck. I tilted my head to the side to give him more access. I then felt light kisses down my neck. I closed my eyes as I enjoyed the moment.

His hand roamed around my body. He skillfully took off my bra, exposing my chest. He touched my hardened nipples and I immediately moaned.

"You're mine Madeline. I don't want any other man to touch you as I do. I am the only one who can do these things to you." I heard him whisper.

I opened my eyes and he picked me up. He took us to the bedroom as he carefully placed me on the bed.

He began to take off his clothes exposing his sexy body. He was extremely fit and had an impressive six-pack. I saw him move closer towards me and he helped me take off my skirt and underwear. Now we were both fully naked.

He got on top of me and began to kiss my chest. I could feel his warm mouth against my skin as he kissed and licked my breasts. He moved lower, kissing my stomach. There was this obvious attraction that Grayson and I had for one another. But it was at times like this that this passion inside us seemed to overflow.

I felt him travel lower until he reached my core. He continued to kiss and suck on the spot like he had done to my breast. His arms held my legs still as he continued to lick and suck my core. He knew how to pleasure me, he was a master at this. The pleasure began to consume me and I knew I was about to reach my climax.

I began to moan once again.

GRAYSON POV

Madeline was so beautiful. I just couldn't get enough of her. Her skin was so soft. Her frame was so small and delicate. I just wanted to devour her and make her mine.

I loved hearing her moan. I loved pleasuring her and touching her in places only I was allowed to. She was mine and I wanted her to know that.

As I tasted her and made her moan I couldn't help but get a hard on. Just hearing her voice was enough to make me go crazy for her. My beautiful Madeline. Only she could make me feel this way. I was madly in love with her and I would make sure to cherish every moment we have together.

MADELINE POV

"I want you Grayson. Please, I need you." I didn't even know what I was asking for. I just needed relief.

Grayson stopped and quickly grabbed a condom from the side table. He put it on and almost immediately I felt him go inside me. He thrust his manhood inside me, making me go wild with pleasure. We then began to kiss.

Before we knew it, we had both reached our climax.

[END OF MATURE SCENE]

We got in the shower after that and then changed into some comfortable clothes. We laid on the comfortable bed and I rested my head on his chest. He wrapped his arm around my waist pulling me closer to him. I felt him place a gentle kiss on my forehead.

"I love you Madeline."

"I love you Grayson."

We just laid there in silence. It felt so comfortable just being beside him. I couldn't explain it but just being in his arms and feeling him near me gave me so much peace. He made me feel safe and I couldn't be happier at this moment.

"I'm sorry for overreacting earlier. It's just that you and Wiliam have a past together that I wasn't a part of. I was just afraid that you would grow feelings for him and leave me."

Grayson broke the silence. I found it sweet that he was apologizing.

"You know, if you ever left me again, I don't think I would be able to take that. I love you too much to see you leave me. I can't help but get possessive of you seeing another man desire you. I want you all to myself."

Grayson hugged me tighter.

I moved back as I faced him.

I began to brush his hair. I realized it was long now. Although it looked good on him. Everything looked good on him.

"Thank you for apologizing." I smiled.

"I will confess. Before I left England and moved back to New York, William told me he was in love with me."

I could see the surprised and almost worried look on Grayson's face.

"But I told him I didn't feel the same way. Even then, I couldn't forget about you. I've never stopped loving you Grayson. If I wanted to be with William I would have dated him a long time ago, but I didn't. You're the only one that makes my heart beat fast whenever you're around. I can't help but miss you when you're not with me and just looking at you brightens up my day. I'm madly in love with you Grayson, and sometimes I worry that I am stuck in a wonderful dream and that at one point I will wake up and you won't be by my side."

I hadn't realized how happy Grayson made me feel. He gave me strength and supported me when I felt down. He was so caring and gentle with me which made me love him even more. I just couldn't help but worry that something else could come and ruin what we had.

I felt Grayson move closer as he pressed his lips against mine. It was a soft warm kiss. I believe it was his way of comforting me.

"I'm happy to know you truly love me. I also don't want to lose you nor what we have right now. I promise I will protect you and make you happy. Thank you for opening up with me. I was being selfish and inconsiderate of your feelings. I will try to control my jealousy. Thank you for being by my side, I really don't deserve you."

Will You Marry Me?

M ADELINE POV

I sat beside Grayson as we prepared to arrive in Paris. I had been looking forward to this trip for a very long time. I knew at some point in my life I would visit Paris. I had always wanted to go there since I was a child.

I was just happy to know that I would get to visit the city of love with the man I love.

Soon we had arrived at our hotel. As we entered our room I practically ran to the balcony to take in the beautiful view of the city. I loved how I could see the Eiffel Tower from here.

"Look Grayson, you can see the Eiffel Tower from here!" I was very excited.

Grayson walked over to me and I felt him embrace me from behind.

"I am so glad to see you this happy."

I turned around to face Grayson and I hugged him back.

"Thank you Grayson for making my dream come true and taking me here."

I felt him kiss my head.

"I love you"

"I love you" I told him.

We put our clothes in the drawers and we headed out to explore the city.

Grayson grabbed my hand and we walked to a Cafe to have lunch. We sat down and quickly ordered.

"I want to take you somewhere special tonight. I'm not going to tell you where it is but we need to be ready by 8."

Grayson was so sweet.

"Now I really want to know where we're going. But I won't ask since it's clearly a surprise. Thank you Grayson." I smiled at him.

"You're so beautiful when you smile."

He pulled my hand to his lips and he kissed it. Grayson was very affectionate and wasn't afraid to show it.

Our food finally came and we ate.

As soon as we were done we walked around the streets of Paris and visited some shops. It was so much fun just being with Grayson. This city was beautiful but I knew it wouldn't have been as fun if I was here with someone else that wasn't Grayson. He made me happy.

We visited the shop Laduree and purchased some macarons. Grayson wasn't a fan of sweets but he knew how excited I was to visit this shop so he bought me a whole box of macarons.

We took pictures together everywhere we went. I truly wanted to treasure these moments.

It was getting late and we needed to get ready for this surprise Grayson had planned for me.

As soon as we arrived at the hotel I began to style my hair and I did my makeup. Luckily I had brought with me an elegant dress just in case we went somewhere special.

I had finally finished getting ready and just in time. Grayson had been busy making some phone calls and getting ready himself he hadn't seen me yet.

As I walked over to him he smiled.

He wrapped his arms around my waist and he pulled me in for a kiss.

"You look beautiful"

"Thank you. You look very handsome in that suit." Grayson looked amazing in everything he wore. He had these beautiful eyes, a handsome face, and the body of a god.

We headed out right after that. We got into a taxi and as soon as I got out I knew where we were heading.

The Eiffel Tower stood before me. We walked to the elevator and we were taken to the top. Grayson had made a reservation for us at a restaurant in the Eiffel Tower.

We were lead to our table. I was so happy to see that we got to sit near the window.

Grayson ordered us some wine and we ordered our food. Our server then left.

"Thank you so much Grayson for doing this. This means a lot to me."

I couldn't believe that he had organized this for us. The view from here was breathtaking. I had always dreamed about visiting the Eiffel Tower and viewing the beautiful city of Paris at night like in the movie Ratatouille. It was my favorite film as a child and now my childhood dreams were coming true thanks to Grayson.

"You're welcome my love. I just want to make you happy. I'm glad I was able to do that today."

He grabbed my hands and kissed them.

Our food came and we ate. We talked about the different museums and locations we planned to visit during our trip. I always had a good time whenever I was with Grayson. He just made everything better.

We finished our food and we left. We both wanted to walk around the Eiffel tower and take in a better view so we decided to go back to our hotel later.

As we walked around Grayson suddenly stopped me and grabbed my hands.

"You are the most beautiful person I know. Sometimes I wonder how I got so lucky to have you by my side. We've known each other our entire lives yet the day we met I knew you were the one for me. I was only a child but even then you made my heart skip a beat. You make me happy and I don't see myself with anyone else but you. I love you Madeline."

He went on one knee and opened up a small box with a beautiful ring.

"Will you marry me?"

Grayson was shaking. I could tell he was nervous.

I felt tears run down my cheeks. I was crying tears of joy.

"Yes!" I answered.

He put the ring on.

He then picked me up and spinned me around as we kissed.

"Be prepared, now that you said yes I don't plan to ever let you go."

I didn't plan on letting him go either.

I then hugged him. I wrapped my arms around his large frame. He hugged me back with the same gentleness.

I couldn't believe it. I was engaged to Grayson Lockwood, the man I love.

The Wedding

The end

MADELINE POV

I stood in front of the mirror and stared at my reflection. I wore a wedding gown and my hair was carefully styled in beautiful curls. Today was the big day. It had been almost a year since we had prepared for this day and it was finally here. I was getting married to the man of my dreams.

"You look beautiful." It was Ian.

He had raised me along with Grace. He had always acted like a father figure and cared for me.

Today he was going to walk me down the aisle as if he were my father.

"Thank you Ian."

I wrapped my arm around his and we headed out to meet the others. The music started and I proceeded to walk down the aisle. As soon as I saw Grayson I felt tears run down my cheeks. He began to cry as well.

Ian gave me a hug and then let me go. I held Grayson's hands and the ceremony began.

Before we knew it we were pronounced husband and wife.

Grayson pulled me toward him and we shared a sweet kiss. We couldn't help but smile at one another.

"You look beautiful." Grayson whispered

I gave him a quick peck on the lips.

Everyone began to cheer and clap.

It was now time for the party. We headed to a limousine and finally arrived at the wedding reception.

Grayson and I had our own special table. People walked over to us to congratulate us on our wedding.

It was finally time for our first dance.

Grayson grabbed my hand and led us to the dance floor.

I wrapped my arms around his neck and he held my waist. I was happy just being in Grayson's arms. I didn't know what the future held for me and Grayson but I knew that together we could get through anything.

CPSIA information can be obtained
at www.ICGtesting.com
Printed in the USA
LVHW031315151222
735289LV00010B/2349